Transform Your Life with NLP

Teach Yourself®

Transform Your Life with NLP

Paul Jenner

For UK order enquiries: please contact Bookpoint Ltd,
130 Milton Park, Abingdon, Oxon OX14 4SB.
Telephone: +44 (0) 1235 827720. Fax: +44 (0) 1235 400454.
Lines are open 09.00–17.00, Monday to Saturday, with a 24-hour
message answering service. Details about our titles and how to
order are available at www.teachyourself.com

For USA order enquiries: please contact McGraw-Hill Customer
Services, PO Box 545, Blacklick, OH 43004-0545, USA.
Telephone: 1-800-722-4726. Fax: 1-614-755-5645.

For Canada order enquiries: please contact McGraw-Hill Ryerson Ltd,
300 Water St, Whitby, Ontario L1N 9B6, Canada.
Telephone: 905 430 5000. Fax: 905 430 5020.

Long renowned as the authoritative source for self-guided
learning – with more than 50 million copies sold worldwide –
the **Teach Yourself** series includes over 500 titles in the fields of
languages, crafts, hobbies, business, computing and education.

British Library Cataloguing in Publication Data: a catalogue record
for this title is available from the British Library.

Library of Congress Catalog Card Number: on file.

First published in UK 2010 by Hodder Education, part of
Hachette UK, 338 Euston Road, London NW1 3BH.

First published in US 2010 by The McGraw-Hill Companies, Inc.

This edition published 2010.

The **Teach Yourself** name is a registered trade mark of
Hodder Headline.

Typeset by MPS Limited, A Macmillan Company.

Printed in Great Britain for Hodder Education, an Hachette UK
Company, 338 Euston Road, London NW1 3BH, by CPI Cox &
Wyman, Reading, Berkshire RG1 8EX.

The publisher has used its best endeavours to ensure that the URLs
for external websites referred to in this book are correct and active
at the time of going to press. However, the publisher and the
author have no responsibility for the websites and can make no
guarantee that a site will remain live or that the content will remain
relevant, decent or appropriate.

Hachette UK's policy is to use papers that are natural, renewable
and recyclable products and made from wood grown in sustainable
forests. The logging and manufacturing processes are expected to
conform to the environmental regulations of the country of origin.

Impression number   10 9 8 7 6 5 4 3 2 1

Year   2014 2013 2012 2011 2010

Acknowledgements

I would like to thank all those who took part in my focus groups to see in what ways they could transform their lives with NLP.

A very special thank you to Victoria Roddam, my editor at Hodder Education.

Image credits

Contents

Meet the author

For years I've been investigating the secrets of human happiness and fulfilment and I know the unconscious mind is the key. But how to get at it? There are all kinds of definitions of NLP (Neuro-Linguistic Programming) but my own informal explanation of what, to me, is NLP's most important idea is that it's sending your unconscious mind to the movies. We all know that a picture is worth a thousand words so why should it be any different for the unconscious? You don't *tell* your unconscious mind what to do. You can't. Instead, you show pictures. The unconscious mind seems to respond to that.

Of course, there was nothing new about visualization when Richard Bandler and John Grinder introduced their ideas in the 1970s. What they did was take the process to a whole new level, drawing on the techniques of the modern cinema, doing everything and anything that might win an Oscar for best director. They made use of the fact that when we run an 'internal movie' we automatically hypnotize ourselves. And in that altered state, the movie itself reprograms the unconscious. So we need to be very careful what we visualize. We can do a lot of good and we can also do a lot of harm.

This isn't a textbook of NLP. You won't find every NLP technique in it. (For that, you might like the companion volume, *Essential NLP*). Instead I've selected the techniques that I think work the best and are the most useful for transforming your life.

Paul Jenner (Spain, 2010)

Only got a minute?

Neuro-Linguistic Programming (NLP) is a collection of techniques to put you in control of your mind. Those techniques include: visualizing scenes as a way of programming the brain; copying the way experts and geniuses do things; using the methods employed by hypnotists in a way specially adapted for everyday life; and establishing rapport by copying body language.

What happened in your past life (and therefore the way you view your present and your future) can be interpreted in a more positive light.

Your learning ability is the key to almost everything in your life.

It's important to stop your inner voice being negative and, instead, convert it to a positive outlook.

If you visualize yourself being more confident then you will become more confident.

If you visualize yourself succeeding at something then you will increase your chance of success.

If you visualize yourself as healthy so you will become more healthy and recover more quickly from illness.

Test your powers of visualization right now by calling up a favourite scene and then manipulating it like a film director. Pull back, zoom in, switch viewpoints, try soft focus, use different lighting effects, employ slow motion, add music – in short, use your creative imagination to the maximum.

You'll be more persuasive if you (a) first establish rapport by copying body language, (b) speak slowly, in time to people's breathing, and (c) plant ideas rather than try to give orders – for example, by telling stories.

You can increase feelings of love by running an internal movie of the most romantic scenes from your life together – and you can fall out of love by running an internal movie of your worst times together.

You can learn to hypnotize anyone who is co-operative.

5 Only got five minutes?

1. NLP basics

Neuro-Linguistic Programming (NLP) is a collection of techniques that can rapidly put you in control of your mind. The main divisions are:

1 Modelling – a special way of copying the skills of geniuses and experts by first of all intuitively absorbing their habits.
2 The Milton Model – a way of using the techniques of the hypnotherapist Milton Erickson in everyday life.
3 Visualization – inducing trance and automatically programming your unconscious at the same time.
4 Interpersonal skills – especially establishing rapport by matching and mirroring other people's body language and way of speaking.

You can easily put yourself into trance using the Betty Erickson method.

There are more than a dozen NLP presuppositions, including 'If one person can do something, anyone can learn to do it' and 'The map is not the territory'.

2. Transform your past

Your past is all about what you choose to remember and how you choose to feel about it.

When thinking back, try changing the qualities (submodalities) of your visualizations in ways that will be positive and helpful.

Forget about things that make you unhappy.

---

3. Transform your learning abilities

If one person can do something then you can also learn to do it – your learning ability is the key to almost everything in your life.

You can accomplish a great deal by modelling yourself on experts, either by being with them or by watching recordings.

---

4. Transform your inner voice

When your inner voice is negative tell it to shut up, or discredit it by making it sound like someone you distrust.

When you're having a problem you can't solve, ask your unconscious to find a solution – it probably will.

---

5. Transform your success

A good time to reprogram your unconscious for success is just before you fall asleep.

When you're feeling anxious about your ability, try visualizing a situation in which you've felt confident and then hold on to that feeling.

Try making successful behaviour automatic by repeatedly linking it to a trigger (known in NLP as an 'anchor').

---

6. Transform your health

Visualization is a powerful health technique. Visualize yourself doing healthy things, visualize yourself giving up unhealthy things and, above all, visualize yourself being healthy.

And don't forget plenty of laughter.

---

7. Transform your powers of persuasion

You'll be more persuasive if you create rapport by copying another person's body language, time your speech to the rhythm of their breathing, and plant ideas with subtle questions, anecdotes and stories rather than giving direct orders (which might create resistance).

---

8. Transform your love life

To increase your romantic feelings, become the director of your own internal romantic movie compiled from happy scenes of your life together.

To increase your romantic allure, visualize yourself behaving in the way you would like.

To decrease your feelings (to get over a break-up), create an internal movie of the five worst things your ex ever did.

9. NLP and hypnosis

NLP derives many of its techniques from hypnotherapy.

We all go into trance every day (when, for example, reading a book). It's not unusual.

When you hypnotize people you simply use trance to help them bring out things they already know.

It's not difficult to hypnotize people if they're willing.

10 Only got ten minutes?

1. NLP basics

Neuro-Linguistic Programming (NLP), founded by Richard Bandler and John Grinder, is a collection of techniques that can rapidly put you in control of your mind.

Modelling, one of four principal divisions within NLP, is a special way of copying the skills of geniuses and experts by first of all intuitively absorbing their habits.

As a result of modelling Milton Erickson, the hypnotherapist, Bandler and Grinder devised the Milton Model, another major division within NLP. The Milton Model, which the two men described as being 'artfully vague', uses hypnotic techniques to influence people in everyday life.

You can easily put yourself into a trance using a simple method that was employed by Erickson's wife Betty, who was also a hypnotherapist. Get comfortable and begin by identifying three things you can actually see, three you can hear and three you can feel where you are. You then identify two different things in each category, then one. You next generate a scene in your imagination and identify one thing you can see, one you can hear and one you can feel. Then you identify two different things in each category, then three. You should now be in trance, but, if not, carry on in the same way until you are.

Visualization is the third main division within NLP. When you visualize something you automatically go into a trance. Therefore, what you visualize easily enters your unconscious. In essence, if you visualize the way you would like to behave then you give your unconscious a blueprint that it will do its best to follow. For the same reason, visualizing failure is an extremely bad idea.

The last of the four main divisions within NLP embraces various interpersonal skills, including establishing rapport. One way of doing that is to copy the other person's body language and way of speaking (known as 'matching' when what you do is an approximation, and 'mirroring' when it's an exact mirror image). But it must be subtle.

There are more than a dozen NLP presuppositions. Some of the most useful are:

1 If one person can do something, anyone can learn to do it.
2 The map is not the territory.
3 The mind and body are parts of the same system.
4 You cannot *not* communicate.
5 Underlying every behavior is a positive intention.
6 If what you are doing isn't working, do something else.
7 There's no such thing as failure, only feedback.

---

2. Transform your past

Your past is not something fixed but is open to interpretation.

You can change the way you feel about your life by changing the qualities (submodalities) of images, making events seem more recent or more distant, changing the context (reframing), and by switching from association to dissociation (seeing bothersome events from an outside perspective).

The Fast Phobia Technique uses double-dissociation to cure phobias.

NLP is more interested in how you *keep* being the way you are, rather than how you got that way.

3. Transform your learning abilities

Your learning ability is the key to almost everything in life.

If one person can do something, anyone can learn to do it.

Modelling means unconsciously *absorbing* what experts do – a process that can be enhanced by inducing a state of flow.

It helps to try to *become* the person you're modelling (first position).

Explicit modelling involves subtracting elements to find out which ones are important.

4. Transform your inner voice

There are various methods of dealing with a negative inner voice, including telling it to shut up, discrediting it by making it sound like someone you distrust, Swishing and reframing.

Our 'internal maps' of the world have defects caused by generalization, by the tendency to make the facts fit what we want to believe, and by the inability of our brains to process all the data.

Six Step Reframing can be used to find better ways of doing things.

5. Transform your success

You can programme yourself as you fall asleep, so you'll wake up feeling positive and optimistic.

When you don't feel very motivated to do something, you can 'borrow' motivation by Swishing it from something else.

The Circle of Confidence involves visualizing a circle on the floor, pouring it full of the confidence you once felt from a previous situation, and then stepping into it.

The New Behaviour Generator involves visualizing yourself as if you were in a film and behaving in that ideal way.

Anchors are things that trigger automatic behaviours. Visualize the behaviour you would like and then set your anchors (preferably one visual, one audible and one kinaesthetic). When you need that behaviour, fire the anchors you created.

It can be better to 'reverse engineer' a goal by working backwards from it, rather than working forwards from where you are now.

---

6. Transform your health

An NLP technique for harnessing the placebo effect involves visualizing yourself as completely recovered.

To create regular, healthy habits, Swish motivation from another enjoyable regular activity, such as taking a shower.

Creating an 'internal movie' showing all the negative effects of something can help you give it up.

Model someone you admire who already has a healthy lifestyle.

The Circle of Health involves visualizing a circle on the floor, pouring into it the excellent health you once experienced, and stepping into it.

To beat stress, get yourself very relaxed and set anchors (see above). Firing the anchors in stressful situations will help you.

Laughter, overloading the brain with tasks, distraction, and self-hypnosis are all ways of helping you to cope with pain.

---

7. Transform your powers of persuasion

Copying another person's body language (known as matching and mirroring) is a way of helping to create the rapport that will make it easier to influence them.

The Milton Model is an aspect of NLP based on the techniques of the hypnotherapist Milton Erickson. One of the techniques is planting ideas by telling stories. Others include presuppositions (speaking and acting as if something has already been decided) and binds, in which someone is presented with limited choices.

Speaking slowly with pauses timed to the rhythm of breathing can give greater weight to the things you say.

---

8. Transform your love life

Making an internal movie of the most romantic scenes from your life together can increase your feelings of love. To recapture that 'walking on air' feeling, visualize a scene from your early days together then abruptly substitute an image of your partner now.

The Circle of Love involves visualizing a circle on the floor, pouring into it the love you felt on a previous occasion, and then stepping into the circle.

Model couples who have had long, happy relationships.

When you have a disagreement, never make things worse by recalling previous disagreements.

The Romantic Behaviour Generator involves creating an internal movie of the way you would like to be.

You can improve your love life by creating anchors that make you feel romantic, or sexy, or more aroused, or less anxious about performance.

To get over a break-up, create an internal movie of the five most dreadful things your ex ever did.

---

9. NLP and hypnosis

Hypnosis is 'the evocation and utilization of unconscious learning'.

The standard technique for hypnotizing someone is to feed their experience back to them before taking them in the direction you wish to go: 'Now, as you sit in that comfortable red chair... your feet... on the floor... your hands... feeling the smoothness... of the armrests... and hearing my voice... so I'd like you to...'.

Signs that you have succeeded in putting someone into trance may include flatter features, changes in breathing, warmer hands, eyes rolled up or closed eyelids flickering.

The purpose of hypnosis should always be agreed at the outset.

1

NLP – the basics

In this chapter you will learn:
- *the most important concepts of NLP*
- *how to practise the basic skills*
- *how to begin using them.*

Experience has a structure.

NLP presupposition

NLP stands for Neuro-Linguistic Programming. Yes, it's quite a mouthful. And somewhat daunting. Which is why most people say simply, 'NLP'.

Various definitions of NLP have been put forward, but the fact is that NLP is *not* a single discipline so much as a collection of quite different techniques. So, in reality, no definition is possible. Nor is there a widely accepted definition of what NLP *does*. So I'm going to give you my own:

NLP is a collection of techniques that can rapidly put you in control of your mind.

Behind NLP is the observation that the things you experience must be organized in your mind in some structured way. Once you understand the structure, you can better control your mind. Once you're in control of your mind, you're in control of your body and your behaviour. You're in control of your life. You have more choices.

How would you feel if, while reading this book, your arm suddenly jerked into the air all on its own? Or your leg abruptly began to swing from side to side? And your head twitched violently? Of course, you'd be aghast. And yet we all accept our minds behaving in exactly that uncontrollable way. We set off to do one task and our minds jump to something quite different. We're about to give a speech, or swing a golf club or set off down a ski run and our minds tell us *we're no good*. A little voice says, 'You're not able to do this.' Trying to go to sleep at night the little voice is at it again: 'You made a mess of things today. No doubt you'll be just as bad tomorrow.'

Have you ever thought of telling the little voice to 'shut up'? Richard Bandler, co-founder of NLP along with John Grinder, often uses that very simple technique himself. But NLP also has many rather more sophisticated ways of controlling and harnessing the unconscious – because it's the unconscious that we're really talking about.

As Bandler puts it, your mind is running all the time and, if you don't make it run in the direction you want to go, it will simply 'run all over the place'. As a young man he went on holiday to Mexico where he saw someone fishing in a lake and decided to have a go as well. Then he saw the signs warning that because of the high mercury levels the fish would be dangerous to eat. He clearly saw an analogy. You shouldn't put sewage into a lake and, similarly, you shouldn't put sewage into your mind. Those negative thoughts, thrown up by the unconscious, are exactly the result of 'pollution'.

NLP can usefully be divided into four main areas:

1 MODELLING

Modelling means discovering what geniuses and experts do that's different from what other people do.

What will this do for me? Once you've isolated the key elements you can learn to achieve the same results as the experts.

2 THE MILTON MODEL

One of the people Bandler and Grinder modelled in the early days was the founding president of the American Society for Clinical Hypnosis, Milton H Erickson. As a result, they developed what's known as the Milton Model, which pins down the linguistic patterns used by Erickson in hypnotherapy.

What will this do for me? By emulating those patterns you can be more effective in your communications with other people.

3 VISUALIZATION

If you visit a hypnotherapist you'll be asked to visualize various things. What Bandler and Grinder did was develop highly sophisticated visualization techniques that people could use either under the direction of an NLP practitioner or *on their own for rapid change*. A better term might be 'internal cinema' because it's not just a question of manipulating images but also sounds and sensations.

What will this do for me? These visualizations can enhance your life in all kinds of ways, from curing phobias to increasing confidence.

4 INTERPERSONAL SKILLS

In addition to the Milton Model, Bandler and Grinder also created a whole range of other techniques for interacting with people.

What will this do for me? These tools can be used to increase rapport, enhance understanding and give greater weight to whatever you wish to say.

Not everything in NLP fits conveniently under one of these headings, but most of it does. In this chapter we'll be looking briefly at each of these areas. Then, as we move on through the book, we'll be looking at the various techniques in more detail and I'll show you how you can use them to improve just about every aspect of your life.

Modelling

We'll start with modelling, because that's how the whole NLP adventure began back in the early 1970s. At that time John Grinder was teaching at the University of California Santa Cruz and Bandler was a fourth-year undergraduate. In the book *Whispering in the Wind*, Grinder recounts how every week Bandler would knock on his door and invite him to attend a group that he, Bandler, was leading in Gestalt Therapy (a style of psychotherapy that stresses the present moment). Each time Grinder would decline, saying he didn't need therapy. It was only after a few weeks that Bandler explained he actually wanted Grinder to 'figure out how to describe' what Bandler and his friend Frank Pucelik were doing as therapists. Bandler was having a lot of success and, according to Grinder, bringing about rapid and profound changes in clients, but he didn't know how to pass on his skills to others.

Grinder, who had a doctorate in transformational linguistics, was intrigued enough to attend the group and was immediately hooked. Grinder and Bandler's collaboration led not only to a detailed analysis of the methods of Fritz Perls (the father of Gestalt Therapy) as employed by Bandler and Pucelik, but also later those of the 'Family Therapist' Virginia Satir. As a result they created the so-called Meta Model and published it in the first NLP book, *The Structure of Magic, Volume 1*.

Jargon buster – meta

The prefix '**meta**' crops up quite a lot in NLP, to mean 'going beyond'. As Bandler and Grinder wrote, '… each of these wizards (Perls and Satir) has a map or model for changing their clients' models of the world…'. Meta also implies change or transcendence. The Meta Model is all about challenging superficial and imprecise ways of talking (and therefore thinking) so as to provoke people into change.

If you were watching one of the world's top golfers, what things would you copy? The way the player holds the club? The body position while addressing the ball? The swing? All of those things, of course. But what about the food the player eats? What about the mental images formed when looking down the fairway? What about the affirmations spoken internally? What about the footwear? What about that little twitch of the shoulder before swinging the club?

Most people wouldn't take any notice of those kinds of things, but one of them might be important. If so, how would you work out which one? NLP modelling has the answers to these sorts of questions.

Here's another special thing about modelling. What would you say if you, as an aspiring musician, were watching the cellist Yo Yo Ma? I'll tell you. *I could never do that*. Isn't that what you'd say? Or if you met a multi-millionaire businessman? *I could never do that*. Or a grandmaster at chess? All together now: *I could never do that*.

Well, NLP doesn't accept that you could never do *that*. NLP believes you can do anything anybody else can do, whether it involves a physical skill, a mental skill or an emotional skill. That's one of NLP's basic beliefs or 'presuppositions'.

Here's a presupposition that relates to modelling:

> *If one person can do something, anyone can learn to do it.*

No, of course it's not literally true in every case. Some people start out with advantages that others do not have. But as a guiding principle it should be a crucial part of your outlook. Once you stop setting limits on what you think you can achieve then you can achieve unlimited things.

HAVE A GO
Just for fun, make a list of the things that, according to you, you 'can't do'. Then write down the reason you 'can't' accomplish that thing. In a third column assess whether the reason is valid or not. I've made some suggestions to get you started.

Things I'm no good at	Why I'm no good	Valid or not
Dancing	I have no sense of rhythm.	Not valid.
Public speaking		
Drawing		
Playing a musical instrument		
Swimming		
Making money		

When we say we can't do something we're almost always right. The reason is simple. If we don't think we can do something we don't make any effort. We don't take lessons. We don't practise. So it becomes a self-fulfilling prophecy.

But the fact is, if other people can dance (and assuming you're able bodied) you *must* be able to dance. There is no valid reason you can't do what other people have done. If other people can swim you *must* be able to swim. If other people can get rich you *must* be able to get rich. It may not be easy. It may require sacrifice. It may take time. But *you can do it*.

How? That's the next question, isn't it? One answer would be to copy people who have already succeeded. Unlike ordinary copying, modelling starts out as an intuitive process. It's important that to begin with you don't ask any questions either internally or out loud. One of the reasons is that the people you're modelling *may not know themselves how they achieve their results*. They may *think* they know. But they could be wrong.

We all have experience of this kind of modelling already. As infants we modelled ourselves on our parents. We observed their expressions and pulled the same faces. We saw their gestures and we did the same things. We watched how they walked and we walked the same way. And all without language. At some point, much later, we rebelled and tried to do everything differently. But we never fully succeeded because that kind of modelling is hard to eradicate. (That's why middle-aged people tend to see themselves turning into their parents.)

We'll be returning to modelling in detail later. For now, here's a little exercise to give you a flavour of the intuitive approach.

HAVE A GO
Watch part of a film featuring an actor who has a very identifiable style – but don't try to describe anything about the actor in words, either out loud or inside your head. Simply *absorb* the actor by watching the clip again and again and again. Then have a go at

mimicking the actor – the style of clothing, the voice, the delivery, the eyes, the way of moving and particularly (this is very important) the tiny little gestures and shifts that in NLP are known as micro-movements.

Insight

One of my hobbies is riding Western style and before going to saddle my horse I'll often watch a bit of a cowboy movie. It not only puts me in the mood but it subtly changes my whole way of being and somehow the ride always goes better.

The Milton Model

For many years, Milton H Erickson (1901–80) was the most famous hypnotherapist in the USA. Once Grinder and Bandler had honed their modelling skills on the techniques of Perls and Satir, he was an obvious target for them.

According to John Grinder's account, given in *Whispering in the Wind*, he and Richard Bandler effectively used Erickson's own hypnotic techniques to persuade the famous hypnotist to see them at a time when he was 'sequestered' with his three closest students and not receiving visitors. Using a book called *Advanced Techniques of Hypnosis and Therapy* (a compilation of Erickson's articles edited by Jay Haley), they learned several techniques of trance induction and tried them out on one another. They then extracted what they thought worked best and compiled a little speech incorporating variations on two 'embedded commands', which were 'Make time now' and 'See us now'.

Jargon buster – embedded commands

Embedded commands are words or phrases that are contained within sentences and which, although unnoticed by the conscious mind, will be picked up by the unconscious as long as they're spoken skilfully. One way of drawing the attention of the unconscious to these embedded words is to lower the voice when speaking them. Try reading out the following sentences, lowering your voice for the words in italics:

> **You can** learn what they did to *be successful.*
> **You can** agree it's healthier to *be a non-smoker.*

Grinder and Bandler then tossed a coin and Grinder won the task of placing the phone call to Erickson. For two and a half minutes he ran through the induction that had been rehearsed, his voice gradually getting slower and slower and 'simply finally stopping'.

There was then half a minute's silence after which Erickson said, 'You boys come over here immediately'.

This incident has now entered the mythology of NLP, but to what extent Erickson was hypnotized is questionable. The fact is that an introduction had already been effected by a mutual friend, the anthropologist Gregory Bateson, on top of which Grinder and Bandler had made a special journey from California to Phoenix, Arizona – where Erickson lived and worked. It would have been hard for anybody to have refused a polite request, especially from serious young men who had demonstrated such commitment.

Whatever happened that day, the result was that over the next ten months Grinder and Bandler began a routine of passing three to four days at a time with Erickson and then returning to California to 'torture anyone who came within hearing distance with the patterning we were obsessively attempting to master'.

There were several important outcomes. Firstly, Grinder and Bandler advanced their modelling skills. Secondly, they were inspired to set about developing simple techniques that could, in some instances, replicate Erickson's results by means of clever visualizations (see below). Thirdly, they identified the key patterns of speech that Erickson used to achieve his remarkable results. These became known as the 'Milton Model' and were detailed in the two-volume work *Patterns of the Hypnotic Techniques of Milton H Erickson*, published in 1975 and 1977.

Erickson believed the unconscious was always listening but that it needed to be spoken to in a special way. Largely self-taught, he developed his speech patterns by trial and error as a way of planting suggestions in the unconscious mind. Normally he would first induce a trance, but these speech patterns can also have a profound effect on people in their usual waking state. You can therefore learn the Milton Model as a way of being more persuasive in everyday life.

Is it unethical to use the Milton Model? In some circumstances it could be. On the other hand, it isn't magic. It doesn't *compel* anyone to do anything. It simply helps you to be a more effective communicator. We strive every day to persuade people of various things. Some of us use reason. Some of us shout. Some of us cajole. Some plead. Some offer inducements, some threats. Often nothing seems to work. The Milton Model is simply a very effective way to communicate – but it should only be used in appropriate circumstances.

The essence of the Milton Model is that it's often 'artfully vague'. That was the phrase used by Bandler and Grinder in their book. In other words, rather than give a direct instruction ('You will do this', 'You will not do that') the Milton Model plants an idea. This seems to be the way the unconscious works best. The other person then takes that idea into the unconscious and works on it, either because the conscious mind isn't even aware of it, or because the conscious mind can't understand it. That person hopefully then comes to the conclusion you wanted and takes the action you wanted, all the time believing he or she is behaving quite independently. Usually Erickson would be working on people in a trance for maximum impact, but the Milton Model can still be very effective on people in a normal waking state.

STORIES AND QUOTES

When we order people to do things, nag, or even ask quite pleasantly, we're likely to encounter varying degrees of resistance. Most people don't like being told what to do. On the other hand, if we tell a story that subtly illustrates the point we're trying to make, then the other person's unconscious extracts the meaning from it. The effect can be quite profound, because when you have to work out something for yourself the solution comes like a revelation and you remember it better than if you'd been told directly.

Insight

A lot of good poetry works in this way. At first you may not understand the poem logically and yet intuitively you get a certain feeling that's very powerful. That's being 'artfully vague'.

Quotes work a little bit like stories. Rather than give a direct instruction yourself – which might create resistance – you instead quote another person, for example: 'As my headmaster used to say, "If a thing's worth doing, it's worth doing badly."'; 'I always remember my grandfather saying to me, "Drink is a weakness."'

PRESUPPOSITIONS

In this context, a presupposition is a way of speaking in which you take certain things for granted, such as that the other person is going to do what you want. Let's say you're a car salesman. Rather than ask, 'Would you like to buy this car?' you instead ask, 'Do you want to take delivery at once or would you prefer to wait until next month?' By presupposing that you've made the sale, you put the customer in the position of having to oppose your will in order to get out of buying the car. Some people find that hard to do. This kind of presupposition is known as a 'double bind'.

PACING AND LEADING

Pacing and leading are standard techniques in hypnosis but they can also be used in everyday life.

When you feed someone's experience back to them, you establish both rapport and trust because the other person knows that everything you say is true. Pacing, done the right way, can also bring on an altered state of consciousness. The hypnotic technique has become well known, for example: 'You're sitting comfortably in that armchair, your hands resting lightly on your knees, your head against a cushion…'. However, verbal pacing in normal life would have to be a lot more ingenious, for example: 'Fred Bloggs, are you going to sit there in that armchair, with that grin on your face, telling me…'.

CAUSE AND EFFECT

This device links two separate statements. The first statement is known to be true and therefore it is more likely that the second statement will also be accepted as true, for example: 'This vehicle has an air-cooled engine and is the most reliable for desert use.' In this example the person being addressed knows the vehicle does, indeed, have an air-cooled engine and believes that, *because of that*, it's reliable in the desert, even though the speaker hasn't actually said so. 'This task calls for a high degree of sensitivity and therefore I'm giving it to you'; this example is a more subtle and convincing way of saying to someone, 'You have great sensitivity'.

PHRASING

Most of the time, Erickson spoke in a soft, gentle, warm and considerate manner, employing a very unusual and very particular way of spacing his words and phrases. Here is a sample of his approach, adapted from transcripts of Erickson's own sessions:

*And those mental images belong to you... and you can
enjoy getting them back. And I think the best way of getting
them back... is doing so by getting one small one and being
completely delighted by it. Not asking for more... but
just enjoying the pleasure... and delight of that one little
memory. And the next thing you know... you'll get another
little memory that will give you a great deal of pleasure...
and delight. And then some day you'll realize... you really
do have all of it. And when one uses the unconscious
mind... one does it... at the rate of speed that belongs to the
unconscious.*

To actually hear Erickson speaking go to www.youtube.com and
enter 'Milton H Erickson' in the search facility.

Self-hypnosis

Erickson sometimes taught clients how to put themselves into
trance so they could continue certain aspects of treatment at
home. The method I'm about to describe now is, however,
attributed not to Erickson but to his wife Betty, who was herself
a hypnotist. (All kinds of comic ideas come to mind at the idea of
two hypnotists living together, but that's another story.)

What is hypnosis? Derren Brown, the TV mentalist says he doesn't
know what hypnotism really is himself. What we can say for sure
is that it's an altered state of consciousness or, more specifically, a
state of consciousness that's different from what we consider to be
our normal waking state – in other words, a trance. Some experts
describe it as an extreme dissociation between the conscious and
the unconscious.

No !

In fact, we all go into trances every day. When you're totally
absorbed in a book or a newspaper and unaware of the things
going on around you, you're in a trance. It's as simple as that.
When you swing a golf club or throw a dart and get almost

exactly the result you want, you're in a trance. When you're making love with your partner, you're in a trance.

Insight

Don't expect to be able to float above the ground rigid as a board. That sort of thing is stage magic. But once you've learned to put yourself into a trance using this technique, you will be able to bring about significant changes to your mind – I've used it successfully for all kinds of things. It's essential, therefore, that with this and other powerful NLP techniques you carry out an 'ecology check' to be quite certain that any changes you're trying to make are beneficial for you and everyone else.

Jargon buster – ecology check

When you reprogram your unconscious mind there may be unforeseen consequences – not only for you but also for everyone around you. Carrying out an **ecology check** involves investigating all the possible ramifications before going ahead. The key questions are:

What will happen if I succeed in making this change?
What won't happen if I succeed in making this change?
What will happen if I don't succeed in making this change?
What won't happen if I don't succeed in making this change?

HAVE A GO
Step 1: Get yourself comfortable in a place you won't be disturbed. It's not a good idea to lie on the bed because you might fall asleep. But you could sit up on the bed supported by pillows, or arrange yourself in a nice, comfy chair.

Step 2: Decide the length of time you wish to spend in self-hypnosis. Initially I'd suggest ten minutes. That should give you enough time to achieve a deep state of trance without feeling anxiety about 'wasting' time or needing to get on with something else.

As you get used to self-hypnosis you can vary the time. For example, if your aim is to relax after a strenuous or demanding day then you might like to enjoy that state for half an hour or more. On the other hand, just before a difficult meeting you might only have five minutes available. So, having got comfortable, you should say something like this: 'I am now going to hypnotize myself for ten minutes.' You might like to append the actual time by adding, '...which means I will come out of self-hypnosis at 19.30 (or whatever).'

Step 3: This is a key step because it's where you state the purpose of your hypnosis. During your initial experiments I'd suggest starting with one of your more minor problems, leaving your biggest problems to be dealt with once you've become proficient in the technique. The exact words aren't important. Something along these lines will do fine: 'I am entering into a state of self-hypnosis so that I can hand over to my unconscious mind the task of...' or, 'I am entering into a trance for the purpose of allowing my unconscious mind to make the adjustments that will help me...'. Whatever you say, make sure it includes the message that you are inviting your *unconscious* to deal with the matter.

Step 4: State how you want to feel when you come out of your trance. It may be you will simply want to experience your 'normal waking state'. It might be you will immediately want to make use of the change your unconscious has made. In that case you might say, for example, '...and as I come out of my trance I will feel full of confidence and ready to take the next step'. Or it may be that you simply want to continue feeling relaxed or even go to sleep.

Step 5: This is the actual process of self-hypnosis. Basically you're going to engage your three main representational systems in turn to bring the trance about. In the first part of the process you will be noting things you can actually see, hear and feel *in the room where you are*. In the second part you will be noting things you can see, hear and feel *in an imaginary scene*.

---

xxx

Figure 1.1 represents the whole process. In the diagram, V = visual system, A = auditory system, and K = kinaesthetic system.

V	V	V		V	
A	A	A		A	
K	K	K		K	
	V	V		V	V
	A	A		A	A
	K	K		K	K
		V		V	V	V
		A		A	A	A
		K		K	K	K
(External)				(Internal)	

Figure 1.1 Summary of the process for self-hypnosis.

In this process some people talk to themselves internally, but I recommend that *you say everything out loud.* For that reason you'll want to be in a private place. You might imagine that you'd 'wake' yourself up but, in fact, the sound of your own voice, done the right way, will intensify the effect. (If, however, speaking out loud doesn't work for you, then by all means speak internally.)

   a *From your comfortable position, look at some small thing in the room in front of you and say out loud what you are looking at. Choose things you can see without moving your head. For example, 'I am looking at the door handle.' Then, without rushing, focus on another small item. For example, 'I am now looking at a glass of water on the table.' Then move on to a third item. For example, 'I am looking at the light switch.' When you have your three visual references, move on to b).*

   b *Switch attention to sounds and, in the same way, note one after another until you have three, each time saying out loud what you're hearing. Then move on to c).*

c *Note things that you can feel with your body. For example, you might say, 'I can feel the seat pressing against my buttocks.' When you have your three, move on.*

d *Now repeat steps a) to c) but with only two items for each sense: two images, two sounds and two feelings. They must be different from the ones you used before.* Speak a little more slowly.

e *Again repeat steps a) to c) but with only one item per sense: one image, one sound and one feeling. Again, they must be different from any that have gone before.* Speak even more slowly.

f *Close your eyes (if they're not already closed) and think of a scene. Any scene will do. It could be the first thing that comes into your head.*

g *Using this imagined scene, go through the same process you already used for the real scene, but beginning with just one example of each of the three senses: one image, one sound and one feeling. When you've done that, increase to two examples and then three. (Three is usually enough, but if you've stipulated a lengthy session you may need to continue with your fantasy scene by going on to name four images, sounds and feelings, or five or even more.) Remember, each example must be different.* You'll probably find you're automatically speaking very slowly now but if not, make a point of slowing your voice down more and more.

h *After the allotted time, you should begin to come out of trance automatically. But it may help to announce, 'I'll count to three and when I reach three I'll be (whatever you said in Step 4).' Don't worry about getting 'stuck' in a trance. That won't happen. You may feel a little woozy for a while. If so, don't drive a car or do anything demanding until you're sure you're okay to do so.*

Insight

This method works by causing your unconscious to deal with the stated purpose of your self-hypnosis all the time you're in trance and, possibly, afterwards too. Of course, if you'd gone

(Contd)

to see a hypnotist he or she would have continued to speak to you in trance for a stronger effect. Later in the book I'll be showing you how you can also do that by augmenting the Betty Erickson method.

If this technique for inducing trance doesn't seem to suit you, here are two variations you can try.

VARIATION 1

After completing the external phase of the Betty Erickson method, close your eyes and visualize yourself, standing in front of you. Watch the rise and fall of your chest and coordinate your actual breathing to it. Then, beginning at the top of your head, relate what you 'see' to your own internal feelings. For example, 'There's tension in my forehead… I'm squinting… I'm clenching my jaw…'. After you've worked down through your entire body, sense which of your hands feels lighter, then say: 'The hand that feels lighter will continue to feel lighter and will float up towards my face with honest unconscious movements, feeling attracted to my face, so that when it touches my face I will sink into a deep trance'. One of your hands should then do just that and, if it does, you will go into trance.

VARIATION 2

If you go into trance easily, then after completing the external phase of the Betty Erickson method, use the same words as in Variation 1 straight away: 'The hand that feels lighter will continue to feel lighter and will float up towards my face with honest unconscious movements, feeling attracted to my face, so that when it touches my face I will sink into a deep trance'. One of your hands should then do just that and, if it does, you will go into trance.

Visualization

NLP uses a great deal of visualization, so it's a skill that, unless you're already very good at it, you'll need to practise. Strictly speaking, the word 'visualization' refers only to 'seeing' images in your 'mind's eye' (that's to say, recalling memories or creating fantasies), but I'm using the term to include things you can imagine hearing and feeling as well. Once you've created your 'internal cinema', you're then going to be manipulating what NLP calls 'submodalities' in various ways.

Jargon buster – submodalities

Later I'll be asking you to make the images you've visualized brighter or darker, bigger or smaller, closer or further away, and so on; to make sounds louder or quieter; to make sensations stronger or weaker. In the jargon of NLP, these kinds of qualities, possessed by internal images, sounds and feelings, are known as **submodalities**.

As you'll now know from the Betty Erickson method (above), visualization is a way of creating a trance. 'Trance' is one of those words that evoke all kinds of exaggerated ideas. In fact, a trance is simply a state that's different from normal consciousness. When you watch television, read a book or daydream, you're in a trance.

When in a trance, it's easier to program your unconscious mind. In NLP the visualization both induces trance and is itself a program. So the very act of visualization *automatically* channels the new program into your unconscious, which is where it needs to be if it is to be effective.

Insight

In order to be successful, it's essential that the visualization techniques in NLP are carried out with sufficient *intensity*. They have to be created with feeling if they're going to release feeling to you later on.

USING SUBMODALITIES

When we're afraid of things we tend to imagine them *big*. For example, if you're afraid of dogs, when you think about them you probably have a dog's face completely filling your 'screen', its huge fangs bared and seeming to be the size of ice picks. When you think of somewhere you don't want to go – perhaps a hospital – you probably have an image that's dreary and colourless. Perhaps the weight of the building bears down on you and you can even smell it. And what happens when you think of something nice? Possibly the colours are warm and vivid.

The concept behind NLP is that you can turn all this back to front. That is, instead of allowing the way you feel to create the submodalities, you deliberately create the submodalities that will make you feel the way you would prefer to be. In other words, instead of seeing the dog full screen you reduce the size. Instead of the hospital being drab, you paint it in vibrant colours.

Most people have probably never given a thought to the submodalities of their internal cinema. So, if that includes you, here's a little exercise.

HAVE A GO
Lie down somewhere comfortable and have a notebook and pen handy.

Conjour up an image of a person you really love. Write down in your notebook the submodalities. For example, is the image in colour or in black and white? Is it vivid or faint? Is it large or small? Is it central or to one side? Can you hear music?

Next, think of someone you really dislike and once again write down the submodalities. Here are some possibilities that may help you:

Visual qualities (submodalities)

- ▶ *colour or black and white*
- ▶ *large or small*
- ▶ *near or far*
- ▶ *bright or dull*

- *moving or still*
- *clear or blurred*

Audio qualities (submodalities)

- *loud or soft*
- *high pitched or low pitched*
- *clear or muffled*
- *near or far*
- *pleasant or unpleasant*

Qualities of feelings (kinaesthetic submodalities)

- *heavy or light*
- *rough or smooth*
- *hot or cold*
- *constant or intermittent*
- *strong or weak*
- *moving or still*
- *intense or faint*
- *sharp or dull*
- *increasing or decreasing heart rate*
- *faster or slower breathing rate*

Once you've got the hang of identifying submodalities, the next step is to begin manipulating them deliberately.

HAVE A GO
Call up one of your favourite daydreams but this time, instead of just watching it, start manipulating it in various ways. Here are some ideas:

- *See the scene through your own eyes.*
- *Switch 'cameras' to see the scene from another person's viewpoint.*
- *Pull back to see everyone in the scene simultaneously.*
- *Make a split screen and show different images side by side.*

- ▶ *Run a section in slow motion.*
- ▶ *Show a series of stills.*
- ▶ *Change 'camera angles'.*
- ▶ *Play some music.*
- ▶ *Play some completely different music.*
- ▶ *Use soft focus.*
- ▶ *Introduce a voiceover.*
- ▶ *Zoom in for a close-up.*
- ▶ *Move in closer still.*
- ▶ *Pull right back so you can now see for miles.*
- ▶ *Turn down the lights.*
- ▶ *Switch from colour to black and white.*
- ▶ *Have a pianist, as in the silent movie days.*
- ▶ *Have the image fill the entire 'screen'.*
- ▶ *Shrink the image to half the screen, then a quarter, then an eighth.*

---xxx---

Manipulating images is a big part of NLP, so the more you practise the more effective you'll be. Don't worry if you can't actually see an image very clearly or for very long. That's how it is for most people.

Each time you manipulate the image ask yourself what effect it has on you. How does it impact your emotions? For example, you might feel:

- ▶ *more/less excited*
- ▶ *more/less involved*
- ▶ *more/less positive*
- ▶ *more/less happy*
- ▶ *more/less afraid.*

The next bit may work for some people but not others. It's useful to know *where* images are in relation to the emotions they evoke. For example, some of you may immediately say that positive images are up to the right and negative images down to the left. If that's the case, then you have a way of manipulating your feelings by moving images to new locations. Others may be completely mystified. If you're not really aware of internal images being in different places, take some time now to experiment with different kinds of scenes that evoke different feelings in you. If you're still unsure of this whole business, try taking an image of someone you love and deliberately put it in different locations. Do some locations feel inappropriate or unnatural? Is there a location where the image seems right? If you still think every kind of image is directly in front of you, try wagging a finger at the image with your eyes closed and then open your eyes to see where you're pointing – you might be surprised. However, if it turns out that all your images are directly in front of you, don't worry. That's perfectly normal.

Insight

Make time to carry out these experiments in submodalities every day. See if you can improve your ability to visualize. If you have to commute by train regularly this is a good way of creatively passing the journey.

SWISHING

Swishing is a famous NLP visualization technique. Essentially it means quickly swapping one image for another so that the submodalities from the first image become transposed to the second image. We'll be seeing how this works later in the book.

SPINNING

NLP treats the body as so intimately connected to the brain as to be an extension of it. When a memory (a visualization) makes you feel light headed, or gutted, or have butterflies in your stomach, or heartbroken, you're identifying ways in which your thoughts manifest themselves in your body.

Here's a question. When you're visualizing something and feeling a particular emotion, *where* in your body do you feel it? And does it *move*? Does it *spin*?

Again, this is a concept that some people relate to and others do not. Try holding your hand out in front of you, or a little to the side, as you talk about a subject and see how it spontaneously moves. It may be better to have someone watch you so you don't have to think about your hand but just let it behave naturally. You may find that your hand moves as if it's spinning something. In that case, note which way it moves when you're talking about something positive and how it moves when you're talking about something negative. In all probability, the two will be different.

Having established which way is positive and which way is negative, you might sometimes be surprised by your hand moving in the 'wrong' direction. For example, it may be that when you're describing something dangerous you actually move your hand in the positive direction. If so, that would be because you feel exhilarated by having escaped or proud of the way you behaved – both positive emotions. Your hand, then, will probably reflect how you feel about the thing, rather than the qualities of the thing itself.

Having identified the phenomenon of spinning, you can now set about controlling it and, by so doing, help to control and direct your emotions. You can spin them faster or slower. In other words, move your hand to reflect the way you want to feel. Even if you didn't find that spinning was something natural to you, you may still find that this has a clear effect. If you go faster you intensify the feeling. If you go slower you reduce it. And, of course, you can try reversing the direction to create the opposite feeling. If it works for you, great; if not, don't worry.

Interpersonal skills

I'm using the heading of 'interpersonal skills' to lump together several important NLP techniques. Many of these also derive from the work of Milton Erickson, who believed that in order to be able to influence someone, he first needed to establish rapport.

Here's a little taster of the methods we'll be learning later in the book. Try to establish rapport with someone you've just met in the following ways.

1 *By matching and mirroring, that is, subtly copying their body language.*

Jargon buster – matching and mirroring

Matching is approximating someone else's body language.
Mirroring means so precisely copying someone else as to seem like a mirror image.
For example: if the other person reclines in a very casual way, you do the same. If they rest their chin on their hands, you do the same. And so on.

---

2 *By subtly copying their way of expressing themselves. In particular, watch out to see if they have a primary representational system, which may be visual, auditory or kinaesthetic and, if so, employ the same kind of language.*

Jargon buster – primary representational system

The **primary representational system** is the preferred way that a person internally experiences or relives something. For many people the primary experience is visual, but others 'think' first in sounds or feelings. A few might lean towards taste and smell – and many more will where food is concerned. The clue is given by the language people use, for example: 'At a *glance* it all looks pretty *clear*'; 'It all *sounds* good to me so I'll get *tuned in*'; 'I'm *feeling lukewarm* about this but let's keep in *touch*'.

---

3 *By repeating what someone has said, before introducing an idea of your own. This is a variation on the techniques of pacing and leading, as described in* The Milton Model *on pages 11–12. For example: 'So you're saying we should go*

somewhere different this year and try new things, such as having a holiday in Morocco. That's a great idea. What about diving in the Caribbean?'

All the time you're doing these things you need to calibrate.

Jargon buster – calibrating

Calibrating means observing someone's body language very closely and relating it to his or her emotional state. For example, you would note tone of voice, skin colour, posture, gestures, micro movements and so on.

If your calibration suggests you're not having the effect you want then you'll obviously have to vary your techniques. (See the presupposition below: If what you are doing isn't working, do something else.)

Presuppositions

Before we leave this discussion on NLP basics we need to look at one last area, the NLP presuppositions. We've already met one of them in the discussion on modelling. Just to remind you, it was:

▶ *If one person can do something, anyone can learn to do it.*

Here are the other main ones:

▶ *The map is not the territory.*
▶ *Everyone lives in their own unique model of the world.*
▶ *Experience has a structure.*
▶ *People already have all the resources they need.*
▶ *The mind and body are parts of the same system.*
▶ *You cannot not communicate.*
▶ *The meaning of your communication is the response you get.*
▶ *Underlying every behaviour is a positive intention.*

- ▸ *People are always making the best choices available to them.*
- ▸ *If what you are doing isn't working, do something else.*
- ▸ *There's no such thing a failure, only feedback.*
- ▸ *People work perfectly.*
- ▸ *The most flexible people have the greatest chance of getting what they want.*
- ▸ *Choice is better than no choice.*

So let's take a look.

THE MAP IS NOT THE TERRITORY

Obviously, a printed map is a representation of reality and not the actual ground itself. We all realize that. Yet most of us probably *do* believe that our 'internal maps' of the world are an accurate reflection of the way the world really is. But they're not. They're simply interpretations. Bandler and Grinder certainly weren't the first to make this observation. The actual presupposition is usually attributed to Alfred Korzybski (1879–1950) but the idea itself goes back a long way.

None of us want to feel we live in a fantasy world. We prefer to believe that we see the world as it really is. But, in fact, a fantasy is closer to the truth. Once you accept that idea, so the whole point of visualization becomes so much more obvious.

Let me ask you a few questions:

- ▸ *Have you ever heard people say they went on holiday somewhere and the local people were unfriendly, and then you went and found the reverse?*
- ▸ *Have you ever heard someone say it's hot when you think it's cold (or vice versa)?*
- ▸ *Have you ever heard someone say something is difficult when you think it's easy (or vice versa)?*
- ▸ *Have you ever drawn attention to something you've seen or heard and yet no one else had noticed it?*

These are just everyday examples to illustrate the fact that, to a certain extent, we all create our own versions of the world.

How is this useful to me? It means that you can, in effect, 'change the world' by changing the way you look at the world. If you're unhappy because you believe 'life is terrible' then why not just change your belief? Why not think about all the marvellous things in the world?

In their book *The Structure of Magic, Volume I*, Bandler and Grinder described how clients would come to them for therapy, worn down by a very negative view of their own lives and life in general. Inevitably the two men would conclude that the 'pain and dissatisfaction' these clients felt was due to the 'limitations' they imposed on themselves by the way they represented the world, and was not due to the world itself (as perceived, that is, by happy people).

This is a key point. Just let the significance of the whole idea sink in. Are you the most attractive person on the planet? Yes, if you believe you are. Is your home the nicest home on the planet? Yes, if you believe it is. Is your job the most interesting job that anyone could do? Yes, if you find it so.

EVERYONE LIVES IN THEIR OWN UNIQUE MODEL OF THE WORLD

Now that we know these internal maps are merely interpretations, we can see that everyone's will be slightly different. Ask six people for an assessment of a politician, a policy, a meal or a book and you'll get six different answers.

How is this useful to me? When you disagree with someone it's helpful to try to understand *their* model of the world. Then you can set about finding a solution that fits *their* model. You may also have greater understanding and acceptance of behaviour that's different from yours.

EXPERIENCE HAS A STRUCTURE

The idea of this is that the information coming from our senses is encoded in a systematic way in our brains, just as computers also have a special way of storing data.

How is this useful to me? Once you understand the way your own mind works, you can set about reprogramming it. Similarly, when you know how someone else encodes their experiences you can relate to them, and influence them, more effectively.

PEOPLE ALREADY HAVE ALL THE RESOURCES THEY NEED

This is linked with the previous presupposition and was an important part of Erickson's philosophy. It doesn't mean that you already know how to play a violin but that you already have within you the building blocks – the mental structures, the reasoning powers, the emotions, the experiences and so on – that will allow you to solve your own problems and achieve what you want. But you have to know how to access those resources.

How is this useful to me? It means you can embark with confidence on anything you want to learn to do, armed with the tools in this book.

THE MIND AND BODY ARE PARTS OF THE SAME SYSTEM

When you think about something that's depressing, you probably drop your shoulders and let your head hang down – your mind affects your body. But if you now go out for an invigorating jog in the sunshine you'll probably feel more optimistic – your body affects your mind. NLP effectively sees the mind as being present not solely in the brain, but throughout the body.

How is this useful to me? It opens up more possibilities for changing your way of thinking and therefore your life. You can influence the state of your body by the way you think, and influence the way you think via the things you do with your body.

YOU CANNOT NOT COMMUNICATE

It's very important to realize that we're all communicating all the time, whether we intend to or not. Even silence is a kind of communication. For example, in once case it might mean 'I don't like you, you bore me', and in another 'I'm very comfortable in your presence'. The right interpretation would depend on other signals, such as body language.

How is this useful to me? When you're with people who are sufficiently sensitive you need to realize that you're telling them all kinds of things about you, even if you hardly say anything. Similarly, by cultivating your own sensitivity, you can learn a lot about other people. For example, by watching to see if they're congruent – with body language and spoken language saying the same things – it's possible to know whether or not they're telling the truth. To be an effective and believable communicator, you need to be congruent yourself.

THE MEANING OF YOUR COMMUNICATION IS THE RESPONSE YOU GET

Most of us sometimes feel frustrated, irritable and even angry when someone, as we see it, misinterprets what we've said. But everyone's 'mental map' is slightly different and the way to judge the effectiveness of your communication is not by what you meant, but by what the other person understood.

How is this useful to me? This presupposition puts the responsibility for clarity firmly on you. If someone else doesn't react in the way you expected, or carries out an instruction in the wrong way, then you have to accept that your communication was faulty and that you need to find a better way of expressing your meaning.

UNDERLYING EVERY BEHAVIOUR IS
A POSITIVE INTENTION

Sometimes it can be very hard to understand other people and why
they do the things they do. This simple concept is the key. In their
own minds, people are always trying to do something positive.
Even the most seemingly negative behaviour can be explained in
this way. Someone might start smoking and risk cancer so as to be
accepted – a positive intention. Someone might drink heavily to
dull the pain of a terrible event – again a positive intention. And of
course, you yourself equally do the things you do with a positive
intent.

How is this useful to me? This is one of the presuppositions that
really can give you a new view of life. What's more, once you
realize that there's a positive intention behind every behaviour,
you can set about uncovering it, and where appropriate, find a
better way of meeting that goal.

PEOPLE ARE ALWAYS MAKING THE BEST
CHOICES AVAILABLE TO THEM

This presupposition, closely related to the previous one, says that
the choices people make seem to them the best available options
at the time. When you look at their situation you may see other
better paths that could have been followed, but either they weren't
aware of those possibilities or they doubted their own ability to
pursue them.

How is this useful to me? You'll improve your understanding of
other people when you accept that they may not have had the
choices available to them that you would have had in the same
circumstances. Similarly, when you give yourself a hard time for
choices you made in the past, you can now see that, in fact, you
made the best choices you could in the circumstances. NLP is all
about increasing choices.

IF WHAT YOU ARE DOING ISN'T WORKING, DO SOMETHING ELSE

When we carry out certain actions or think certain thoughts we get specific results. And if we repeat those actions or thoughts we usually get the same results again. Nothing very surprising about that. And if we're happy with these results, all well and good. But supposing we're not happy?

A comic example is that, when trying to communicate with someone who doesn't speak the language, we tend to repeat the same words again and again, but louder and louder. Of course, a better solution is to find a new way – in this case, different words and signs. Some versions of this presupposition add the words 'Do anything else'; anything else must be better than something that doesn't work. As Richard Bandler says, there are things that can seem like great ideas but if they don't actually work then you have to throw them out along with the square wheels.

How is this useful to me? This speeds everything up enormously. You no longer waste time repeating mistakes but immediately seek better ways of doing things.

THERE'S NO SUCH THING A FAILURE, ONLY FEEDBACK

The NLP outlook is that we should all behave like infants who seem to have no sense of failure. They simply keep trying and trying – to crawl, to walk, to speak – until they succeed. The concept of failure seems to be something that develops later in life and so often holds us back. History is full of famous men and women who triumphed only after many setbacks.

How is this useful to me? If you prefer not to attempt things in case you 'fail' then you're severely curtailing the opportunities available to you. Instead, look upon each attempt as a way of getting feedback about what doesn't work and, by a process of elimination, what does. Never think in terms of 'failure'.

PEOPLE WORK PERFECTLY

Self-esteem is very important in NLP, which always aims to see people in a positive way. Someone who spends a lot of time lying around doing nothing would be seen as an expert in relaxation. Someone who is very shy would be seen as an expert in enjoying solitude, and so on.

How is this useful to me? It's important not to label other people or yourself with negative tags, otherwise there's a danger of believing them.

THE MOST FLEXIBLE PEOPLE HAVE THE GREATEST CHANCE OF GETTING WHAT THEY WANT

Look around in nature. The creatures that are the most adaptable are the most numerous and successful. If, like a panda, you insist on eating a special kind of bamboo and nothing else, then you're in danger of extinction.

How is this useful to me? It's important to be able to adapt to changing circumstances, especially in our high-speed world.

CHOICE IS BETTER THAN NO CHOICE

If you always react in the same negative way to a certain kind of situation then, effectively, you have no choice.

How is this useful to me? One of the fundamental aims of NLP is to provide you with more choices of action – more freedom – than you have now, so that you don't have to live like an automaton.

We'll be encountering these presuppositions in various contexts as we move through the book. But they also make useful sayings that you can repeat to yourself in the manner of affirmations. For example, when you doubt your ability to do something you can repeat: 'I have all the resources I need' or, 'Other people can do this so I can learn to do it'. And when you're frustrated by your inability to understand the actions of someone close to you it may help to remember that 'Everyone lives in their own unique model of the world' as well as, 'Underlying every behaviour is a positive intention'.

HAVE A GO
Memorize the presuppositions and use them as affirmations to guide you.

10 THINGS TO REMEMBER

1 NLP is a collection of techniques to put you in control of your mind.

2 When that 'little voice' is being negative, you can simply tell it to 'shut up'.

3 NLP can be divided into four main areas – modelling, the Milton Model, visualization and interpersonal skills.

4 Modelling is a special way of copying the skills of geniuses and experts by first of all intuitively absorbing their habits.

5 The unconscious is always listening but it needs to be spoken to in a special way.

6 You can easily put yourself into a trance using the Betty Erickson method.

7 Visualization both induces trance and automatically programs the unconscious.

8 By altering the qualities of visualizations you can change the way you feel about things.

9 You can establish rapport by copying another person's body language and way of speaking.

10 The presuppositions – the ideas underpinning NLP – can also be used as affirmations.

HOW AM I GETTING ON?

▶ When that 'little voice' has been negative, have you
  successfully told it to 'shut up'?

▶ Have you had a go at modelling someone else?

▶ Have you been able to influence anybody using the Milton
  Model? _Imbeds_

▶ Have you succeeded in putting yourself into a trance?

▶ Have you been able to change the submodalities of a
  visualization?

▶ Have you been able to spin a feeling faster and slower and
  in reverse?

▶ Have you improved rapport with someone else through body
  language, speech, and by pacing and leading?

▶ Have you found that any of the presuppositions appeal to you
  as 'proverbs'?

It's great fun trying out these basic NLP skills and you're going
to be needing them more and more as the book progresses.
So if you weren't able to answer 'Yes' to at least five of the
above questions, look again at the relevant parts of the chapter
and do the practical exercises.

2

Transform your past

In this chapter you will learn:
- *how to forget unpleasant memories*
- *how to rewrite the past*
- *how to turn failure into feedback*
- *how to deal with anxieties, fears and phobias.*

Everyone lives in their own unique model of the world.

NLP presupposition

When you look back on your life so far, it probably appears to tell a story. Quite likely it will seem to you that your present situation was inevitable; that it was more or less predetermined from the very start. Everything seems to lead, step by step, to where you are now.

If you're happy with all of those past steps and where they've brought you, all well and good. You can skip this chapter. But most of us have things in our pasts that bother us. Mistakes we made that keep coming back to haunt us in bed at night. Opportunities we missed. Things other people did to us. Many people find it difficult to be happy *right now* because of the past. And as for the future, the past can seem like a ball and chain forever holding us back. Just as the present seems to be like a stop on a straight railway line from the past, so the future looks to be nothing more than an extension of the same trajectory. But it doesn't have to be that way.

You may think of your past life as something fixed and unchangeable. But it isn't. We can go back and change those steps. We can unlock that ball and chain. We can change that trajectory. In doing so we can make you feel better right now and give you a new future.

Maybe you find that hard to imagine. After all, your past is a fact. Isn't it? Wouldn't changing the facts simply be *lying*? Well, if you've ever studied history you've probably noticed that different historians take quite different views. They study the same time and place but uncover different information and come up with different interpretations. You can do the same. You can:

▶ *ignore anything in the past you wish to*
▶ *put a different interpretation on the past events you choose to remember*
▶ *turn the past, whatever it was like, into a resource that can provide you with a better future.*

Timelines

I should point out straight away that NLP isn't, in fact, very much concerned with the past. Not, that is, in the sense of delving back into your childhood to discover what events, traumatic or otherwise, have made you the person you are today. The approach is completely different from those kinds of therapies in which you might spend months or even years trying to uncover the incidents that have shaped your outlook. As Richard Bandler puts it, he doesn't need to understand *how* you became the way you are, he only needs to understand how you *keep* being that way. As he's fond of observing, the great thing about the past is that it's over.

In their book *Trance-formations*, Bandler and Grinder relate the case of two young women who were abducted together. One remembered everything vividly and was described as a 'psychological mess' as a result. The other had complete amnesia and was 'fine'. The NLP co-founders make the point that, in these kinds of cases, you need to consider very carefully 'whether there is any point to... knowing what happened'. If there isn't, recovering the memory 'may only give... pain'.

Let me ask you a few simple questions. What were you doing this time last week? What were you wearing? What did you eat for dinner on the second night of your holiday last year? What mark did you get in the end-of-term maths test when you were 16? I needn't labour the point. You have forgotten the vast majority of your past life. It may all be in your brain somewhere. It may have an impact on you now. But you can't consciously remember it. What you think of as your past life is nothing more than the small selection of events that you *choose* to remember.

When you tell someone else about your past, no matter how honest you think you're being, you can't do anything other than provide them with a distortion. This is a point we'll return to later in the book in a different context. But, for now, let's just stick with the idea that what you think of as your past is nothing more than a construction of things that you have chosen. Someone else, looking at your life so far, might select quite different facts as being more truly representative.

So let's look afresh at your personal history right now. Let's deselect any past events that are bothering you and let's, as it were, replace them with memories that are more positive. I emphasize that in this exercise we're not going to be altering any facts, so you don't have to be concerned about 'lying' to yourself or anybody else.

The first thing we need to do is discover your timelines.

Jargon buster – timelines

The way you code the pictures, smells, sounds, feelings and tastes from the past, as well as those you anticipate in the future, is known in NLP as a **timeline**.

The way to discover your timeline is to think of something neutral that you've done quite often and will continue to do in the future. That's to say, a regular activity that doesn't arouse strong feelings one way or the other. It could be cleaning your teeth, eating breakfast or going to the cinema, for example.

Think of an occasion when you did that thing very recently, when you did it a month ago, a year ago, two years ago and five years ago. Then imagine doing it in the future, next week, next month, next year, in two years and in five years. Now put each of those scenes into a small picture frame or onto a playing card and imagine them all at once.

Here's the key question. How are those little pictures arranged in your mind's eye? Do you see them scattered randomly all about or do you order them in some way? Most likely you order them, either according to 'through time' or 'in time'.

Jargon buster – 'through time' and 'in time'

▶ *You have the pictures arranged in a straight line running across your vision with the oldest memories on the extreme left and the distant future on your extreme right. In NLP jargon, this is known as* 'through time'.
▶ *You have the pictures arranged in front of you in a V-shape, with the oldest memories on the left at the far end of one limb of the V and the distant future on your right at the far end of the other limb of the V. In this case the present is represented at the point of the V, right in front of your face. This is also known as* 'through time'.
▶ *Your timeline is straight, with your memories behind you and your future in front of you. In NLP jargon this is known as* 'in time'.

Learning to forget

Generally speaking, we forget as time passes. Everything becomes less vivid and less able to impact on our emotions. But, of course, there are exceptions. The elderly often remember childhood incidents more accurately than things that happened a week ago. And when it comes to traumatic events, we relive those experiences as if they were happening right now. In effect, we repeatedly take them out of the timeline and replace them in today's position, right in front of our faces. As a result their impact never lessens. This is a lovely thing to do with nice memories but the worst possible thing with bad ones.

What we're going to do now is reverse the process. We're going to take unpleasant memories and move them further away. That's to say, we're going to take them out of sequence.

Let's say you have a painful memory that won't leave you alone. In that case, what you need to do is move it to the farthest end of your timeline.

HAVE A GO
Step 1: Compare the submodalities of recent and distant memories. (Submodalities are qualities – if you've forgotten about them, refer back to Chapter 1.) For example, recent memories might be in bright colours while distant memories are in pastels, black and white or perhaps sepia-tones. Maybe speaking voices from the past sound 'old-fashioned' or crackly. What about physical sensations? Possibly they're less sharp and more fuzzy.

Step 2: Envisage your timeline and find the memory on it.

Step 3: Lift out that memory, like removing one card from a card file.

Step 4: Now begin changing the qualities of the experience from those of a recent event to those of an event from the distant past. It may help to exaggerate the submodalities that make the experience seem very old. At the same time, steadily move the memory to the *far end* of your timeline of the past. In other words, if you're 'through time' you'll be pushing the memory away to your left. Naturally, the picture will become smaller and smaller and less and less distinct.

Step 5: The bad experience is now just a speck in the distance at the far end of your timeline. As a consequence, you can no longer make out anything about it, nor hear anything.

Step 6: Run through the procedure again and again until the memory no longer bothers you.

Insight

Never again position the painful incident right in front of your face. If something happens one day to force you to think about the subject again, keep it very tiny and push it to the far end of your timeline as quickly as possible. If necessary, repeat the whole process.

The same timeline procedure can be used to retrieve positive memories, dust them off, and line them up, one after another, as a continuous and readily accessible sequence.

HAVE A GO

Step 1: Float back along your timeline looking for a pleasant memory.

Step 2: Lift out that memory, like removing one card from a card file.

Step 3: Now begin changing the qualities of the experience from those of a past event to those of an event that's just happened (see the previous exercise). At the same time, steadily bring the memory to the *near end* of your timeline right in front of your face.

Step 4: Enjoy the memory. Play it over and over, each time recovering more and more information.

Step 5: When you're satisfied, file the memory permanently in its new place, then float back along the timeline, select another memory and repeat the process.

You can carry out this procedure simply for the pleasure of it. But you can also use it, together with the previous one, to assemble memories for a specific purpose. For example, you could collect together all your memories of academic success and de-select memories of those times you didn't do as well as you would have liked. You will then have a record of high academic achievement with which to give yourself confidence for the future. And it will be *factually correct*.

Insight

It would be a good idea to ask yourself *why* you choose the memories you do. Or why you *allow* negative and unpleasant memories to enter your mind. As I'll be emphasizing over and over, NLP is all about taking control of your mind and making it work *for* you, not *against* you.

Learning to see your past differently

The visualizations we've just completed are designed to help you forget the negative and remember the positive. But supposing there are things that bother you and yet you don't actually want to forget entirely? Maybe you think that you were weak, or unreasonable or inept? And that sort of negative self-evaluation lowers your self-esteem today. Nevertheless, you don't want to consign those chunks of experience to the end of your timeline because they have things to teach you and, anyway, they remain an important part of your life.

In NLP you can retain memories but see them very differently through a process known as reframing.

Jargon buster – reframing

Reframing is changing the meaning of something that's happened so you feel differently about it.

Whatever is happening, we're always trying to make sense of it. We try to put it into a context. We try to understand what it means. If we see somebody running, we try to work out why. We look for clues as to whether they're keeping fit, late for an appointment or fleeing a maniac who, if we're unlucky, might focus on us instead.

Do you remember when, as a child, your father was rather irritable with you, and your mother then tried to make you feel better? What did she say? Probably, 'Daddy didn't mean it – he's had a hard day and is feeling tired.'

That was an example of reframing. Your original interpretation was, 'Daddy doesn't love me.' Then your mother changed it into, 'Daddy does love me – he just doesn't feel very good at the moment.'

HAVE A GO
Consider the following situations and reframe them in a more positive way:

- *Sue and Jasmine were giggling together in a corner – I'm sure they were having a joke at my expense.*
- *The boss came in this morning and didn't say a word to me – I think he's going to sack me.*
- *My partner didn't want to make love last night – I think he/she isn't turned on by me any more.*
- *I didn't get the highest grade in my exam – I'm a failure.*
- *I come from a poor background – therefore I'm a worthless person.*

——————————— xxx ———————————

In order to be happy, feel optimistic and behave positively, we need to reframe things in ways that are most advantageous to us. When people are giggling in a corner we can join in. When the boss isn't talking it could be that she or he has personal worries. When your partner isn't in the mood, the headache could be genuine. Passing an exam with less than the highest grade is still an achievement.

And someone who progresses from a poor background has more reason to be proud than someone who started out with advantages.

Sometimes, however, the only believable reframing is that the experience has taught us a useful lesson.

The Decision Destroyer

The visualization that follows is something I've adapted from a standard NLP procedure known as the 'Decision Destroyer' (because it neutralizes poor decisions made in the past). You can use it whenever you can't see how an experience could be reframed in a more positive way.

Step 1: First, put yourself in the right state of mind. In NLP jargon this is called retrieving a 'positive imprint memory' or an 'empowering memory'. In practice it means thinking back to a time when you had the sort of feelings that would have served you well in the situation you're now unhappy about. NLP practitioners usually suggest retrieving a feeling of confidence, but for this exercise I'm going to suggest you search for feelings of capability, benevolence and humour – the way you might feel if a small child came to you with what seemed an overwhelming problem but which you could easily solve.

Step 2: Now intensify those feelings. You can do that by emphasizing the positive submodalities (for example, stronger colours or a bigger picture) and by 'spinning' the feelings, as we saw in Chapter 1. Crank your hand round and round if it helps. Continue like this until you really can feel that positivity.

Step 3: Glide back over your timeline until you find a memory or sequence of memories you want to feel differently about. I emphasize that these are memories you want to keep but aspects of which nevertheless bother you – don't do this with memories you'd prefer to forget. Now look at yourself in this memory and – with those feelings of capability, benevolence and humour to the forefront – *absolve* yourself. Realize that you were younger and less experienced then. Remember the presupposition, 'There's no such thing as failure, only feedback'.

Step 4: Return to the present with the feedback and be grateful you can use that feedback in a positive way.

Step 5: Put the feedback to work for you, your partner, your relatives and your friends.

Insight

We *all* make mistakes *every* day. Even people whom history describes as the greatest men and women of all time made *plenty* of mistakes. The important thing is to *learn* from mistakes, to be *grateful* to have had the opportunity to do so, and then to move forward with the benefit of experience. The English poet, artist and mystic William Blake (1757–1827) clearly understood all about reframing when he wrote these two proverbs:

The road of excess leads to the palace of wisdom.
If the fool would persist in his folly he would become wise.

Dealing with anxieties, fears and phobias

Fear is a very useful invention. It's what stops us from doing all kinds of stupid things that would result in injury or even death. But the programming of the mechanism can sometimes go wrong. When that happens we start to get anxious and fearful about things that actually aren't very dangerous at all. In some cases we can even develop an uncontrollable dread of things that are utterly harmless. Those dreads are called phobias.

If you live in England and have a fear of spiders then that's a phobia. Although you're consciously aware of the fear, its seat is not in the conscious mind. If it were, you'd easily be able to reason your way out of it. You'd recall that British spiders are not poisonous as far as humans are concerned. You'd note that a spider is tiny compared with a person. You'd reason that, although there are spiders everywhere, no spider has ever harmed you in any way. But if you have a phobia, rational thoughts such as these do little or nothing.

When a phobia is caused by *a specific incident in your past* then NLP has a powerful method of dealing with it. It's called, very simply, the Fast Phobia Technique. If you fell into a pond when you were a child and are now afraid to go swimming, or if you were bitten by a dog and are now afraid to touch dogs, or if you once broke your leg on some ice and are now scared to try any winter sports, then this is the technique for you.

When Richard Bandler was designing this technique, he set about discovering what was going on in the heads of people who were afraid and, more important, what was going on in the heads of people who weren't afraid. And he discovered, not surprisingly, that people with phobias imagined terrible things happening to them *vividly*, and people without phobias didn't imagine them.

You may think you're scared of spiders. You may think you're scared of heights. You may think you're scared of dogs. But you're not. What you're really scared of is the image you create in your own mind. That's what scares you. It's the fantasy not the reality that's the problem.

NLP teaches that most problems are created by our imaginations and are therefore imaginary. So the solutions can also be 'imaginary'. That's to say, worked on in the imagination.

HAVE A GO
Think of something that makes you anxious. In this example I'm going to use a visit to the dentist. But you can substitute any other scene you want. Then visualize it from *multiple perspectives*, moving from *first* to *second* to *third* position, and from *association* to *dissociation*.

Step 1: Visualize the scene from *first position* (that is, through your own eyes). See the lights above you... the chair tipping back as the dentist prepares for work... the surgical gloves probing... the noise of the drill... the smell of burning enamel... Conjure it all up as vividly as you can. How do you feel?

Step 2: Visualize the scene from *second position* (that is, through the eyes of someone else involved). The scenario is the same but this time you're taking the role of the dentist. Go through the whole thing again from this new perspective. Maybe the dentist also has problems. Maybe this is a difficult procedure. Maybe your teeth look less than perfect. How do you, as the dentist, feel?

Step 3: Visualize the scene from *third position* (that is, through the eyes of a detached observer). The scenario is still the same but this time you're neither the patient nor the dentist. You don't have to do anything nor have anything done to you. In fact, you're watching from a little distance away. How do you, as an uninvolved observer, feel? Maybe you could move back behind a one-way mirror? How does that feel? Maybe you could go to a building opposite and watch from there. How does that feel?

xxx

Some people are naturally very good at adopting multiple perspectives while others will need to make an effort. There are good reasons for acquiring this habit. One of them is the ability to *associate* with others and to *dissociate* from yourself.

Jargon buster – association and dissociation

▶ **Association** *is to see, hear, touch, taste and smell everything from the perspective of a particular person and, above all, to respond emotionally as that person. Normally we associate with ourselves when we imagine things (first position), but it's also possible to associate with any other person in the scene (second position). This leads to empathy.*

▶ **Dissociation** *is to stand back and not feel directly involved. We can dissociate from ourselves and everybody else by visualizing a scene through the eyes of someone completely uninvolved (third position). In that case, the emotional response will be far less.*

▶ *Dissociation means stepping back and seeing yourself or the situation from outside.* **Double-dissociation** *means stepping even further back and watching yourself, as it were, watching yourself, so you feel even more removed and even safer emotionally.*

The Fast Phobia Technique

The point of the above exercise is to get you used to the idea of changing perspectives. You should now have found that when you move to third position and dissociate, so you don't feel things so strongly. In the Fast Phobia Technique that follows we're going to be revisiting the incident that caused your phobia in the first place. But you don't want to make yourself scared all over again, so we're not just going to dissociate, we're going to *double-dissociate*.

HAVE A GO
Step 1: Imagine that you're in a cinema. In this cinema you're going to be in as many as three places at once – appearing in the film,

watching it as a customer and working as the projectionist, all at the same time. (That's the wonderful thing about the imagination – you can do anything you like.)

Step 2: Be a customer sitting in the cinema, watching a still black and white image of yourself on the screen the moment *before* you experienced this fear for the very first time. (If you can't remember when you first had the fear, instead use an image of the moment before you experienced the fear the most intensely.)

Step 3: Now you're going to become the projectionist sitting in the projection booth. As the projectionist, you can now see yourself in the cinema as well as the image on screen.

Step 4: Still as the projectionist, you run the black and white movie of the frightening situation. You see everything but it means almost nothing to you because you're just the projectionist, sitting in the safety of your projection booth. When you get to the end of the movie, where the person in the film (you) is safe again, you stop the projector and freeze-frame.

Step 5: This is where things get really tricky. You have to leave the projection booth and step into the still picture on the screen. It now turns to full colour and as it does so, the movie runs backwards very quickly. In other words, everyone walks backwards and talks backwards. So it should all look and sound quite funny – and to underline how laughable it is you need to have a film score of comical music (the sort of thing you might hear at the circus). Hearing this music and the backwards voices and seeing the ridiculous movements, *laugh*.

Step 6: Repeat the backwards film sequence several more times, getting faster and faster each time.

——————————————— **xxx** ———————————————

Richard Bandler points out that if you can learn to be afraid in just a few seconds then you can learn *not* to be afraid in just a few seconds. He claims he's never failed with this technique. But you don't have the experience of Richard Bandler so you may have to be prepared to carry out the procedure a few times. If, after completing the six steps, the object of your fear still scores a three or higher on a scale of one to ten, repeat the procedure. If you rate it from zero to two, then go out in the real world and see what happens.

INCREASING THE IMPACT OF THE FAST PHOBIA TECHNIQUE

Just because you have a phobia doesn't mean that you're necessarily very motivated to do anything about it. A lot of phobias are quite easy to live with. If you have a fear of heights, for example, or dogs, or swimming pools you can fairly easily keep away from them. Here's a way of goading yourself into performing the Fast Phobia Technique properly.

Think back to times you came face to face with your phobia *and were embarrassed by the way you behaved*. Try to think of five such occasions and then run them continuously in your mind, one after the other. Five encounters with spiders, five encounters with heights, five encounters with confined spaces, or whatever it might be. Then run those scenes again with everything magnified – make the pictures larger, the colours brighter and the sounds louder. And then run them a third time, very fast, with even greater magnification. Keep running that loop of five scenes until you really feel that the whole phobia thing has so ruined your life that you're desperate to put an end to it. That's the state of mind in which you should approach the Fast Phobia Technique.

Now let's look at the things you can do *after* employing the Fast Phobia Technique.

Richard Bandler has written in his book *Get The Life You Want* that, after running the technique, readers should get up from their chairs 'and test it, and test it, and test it' and that 'bit by bit' the phobia will disappear.

At the time of writing you can see him in action on YouTube in a two-part video called *The Hypnotist*. In this he treats a woman distressed by what she believes is a phobia about flying brought on by a hijacking 27 years earlier. (In fact, Bandler diagnoses her not as suffering from a phobia but from panic attacks brought on by any enclosed environment and, indeed, that proves to be the case.)

Bandler augments the Fast Phobia Technique with three other methods. He employs spinning (see Chapter 1) and hypnosis (see Chapter 9) and then takes her out for desensitization by gradual exposure. He has her ride in a lift with other people, a situation she normally finds overwhelming. From there he takes her to a cinema. (This also has the effect of piling on the pressure and increasing her motivation, as described above.) The final test is to take a flight. During this, the patient again suffers a panic attack but overcomes it.

So it was a success for NLP but not an instant success and, realistically, you shouldn't expect to do better on yourself than Richard Bandler did.

Insight

Whenever you're desensitizing yourself through gradual exposure, it helps enormously to have a laugh. Take some friends with you, having first primed them to kid around, tell jokes, tickle you and generally divert your conscious attention from your fears.

SELF-HYPNOSIS FOR PHOBIAS

Where Richard Bandler used hypnosis, you could substitute self-hypnosis. Study once again the Betty Erickson method described in Chapter 1. Do everything as described, but in Step 3 state the purpose of your self-hypnosis as: 'I am entering into a state of self-hypnosis for the purpose of allowing my unconscious mind to make the adjustments that will help me enjoy the company of dogs/feel relaxed in the presence of spiders/feel comfortable in planes (or whatever it might be).'

10 THINGS TO REMEMBER

1   *Your past is open to interpretation – it can be more positive than you think.*

2   *The problem with past traumas is that we tend to think of them every day, as if they've just happened.*

3   *You can reduce the impact of unpleasant memories by changing their submodalities and pushing them to the far end of your timeline.*

4   *It's often unnecessary to know why you became the way you are; more important is to know how you keep on being that way.*

5   *You can use the 'Decision Destroyer' to feel better about times in the past when you didn't act as you would have liked.*

6   *Reframing enables you to see past events in a more positive, less troubling way.*

7   *You can visualize any past event from multiple perspectives: first position means through your own eyes, second position means through the eyes of another person present and third position means through the eyes of an uninvolved outsider.*

8   *You can reduce the emotional impact of past events by switching to third position and dissociating.*

9   *The Fast Phobia Technique uses double-dissociation and can remove a fear caused by an incident in the past.*

10 *You can augment the effect of the Fast Phobia Technique through self-hypnosis.*

HOW AM I GETTING ON?

▶ *Have you discovered whether you're 'through time' or 'in time'?*

▶ *Have you been able to manipulate your timeline and move an unpleasant memory to the distant past?*

▶ *If so, has that unpleasant memory lost its power?*

▶ *Have you been able to transform past failures into feedback?*

▶ *Have you been able to reframe events that have been bothering you?*

▶ *Have you tried viewing events from multiple perspectives?*

▶ *Have you succeeded in reducing the emotional impact of a past event by switching to third position and dissociating?*

▶ *Assuming you had an anxiety or phobia caused by a past event, were you able to relieve it using the Fast Phobia Technique?*

If you answered 'No' to more than three questions then go back and re-read the relevant parts of the chapter. You need to be proficient in these techniques before you move on.

3

Transform your learning abilities

In this chapter you will learn:
* *how to acquire any skill or knowledge you want*
* *how to model the habits of successful people*
* *how to engage your unconscious mind.*

> *If one person can do something, anyone can learn to do it.*
>
> NLP presupposition

Education is *everything*.

Yes, it can sound rather boring. A stage of your life you thought you'd left behind along with school uniforms and tedious rules.

But there is another way of looking at it. Supposing you had the ability to do anything and everything you ever wanted? Wouldn't life be incredible? Every day would be a great adventure. Each morning you'd wake up and ask yourself what new skill you were going to master next. Acting? Ballroom dancing? Calligraphy? Drawing? A foreign language? Geology? Horse riding? A musical instrument? Sailing? Share trading? Tantric sex? Zen?

How endlessly fascinating life would be! How fascinating *you* would be!

Well, it can be that way. And you already know the NLP presupposition:

> *Anything anyone else can do, you can do.*

And yet, so often, trying to learn a new skill ends not in exhilaration but frustration. In this chapter we're going to change that.

Bandler and Grinder believe that very often we don't get the results we hope for because the experts from whom we're trying to learn *don't themselves know how they achieve their results*. And because of that, the teachers who act as intermediaries between the experts and the rest of us can't teach effectively.

The primary NLP solution to this is modelling, which we first encountered in Chapter 1.

Modelling

'In reading this book,' wrote Milton Erickson, 'I've learned a great deal about the things that I've done without knowing about them.'

The book he was referring to, *Patterns of the Hypnotic Techniques of Milton H. Erickson*, not only brought the techniques of hypnotherapy to a wider audience, but also the modelling methods used by Bandler and Grinder in writing the book.

Modelling is, indeed, all about discovering the things experts and geniuses do 'without knowing about them'. In the words of John Grinder and Carmen Bostic St Clair in *Whispering in the Wind*, it's 'the mapping of tacit knowledge onto an explicit model' and a 'technology whose specific subject matter is the set of differences that make the difference between the performance of geniuses and that of average performers in the same field or activity'.

It's primary focus, then, is *those who teach teachers*. But there's a great deal within the methodology that can help you transform your learning abilities and, therefore, your life.

Broadly speaking there are two stages to the modelling process, implicit and explicit.

Jargon buster – implicit and explicit modelling

Implicit modelling means unconsciously *absorbing* what someone else does, without asking questions and without applying verbal descriptions.

Explicit modelling means consciously deducing which of the expert's actions you've now absorbed are important and which are irrelevant.

Insight

Why not ask questions during the implicit modelling phase? As related in *Frogs Into Princes*, Bandler and Grinder would ask the therapists why, for example, they were touching their clients in a certain way, or shifting the tone of their voices at a certain point. Inevitably the therapists would say they had no idea they were doing those things, let alone why. As a result, the two modellers paid 'very little attention to what people *say* they do and a great deal of attention to what they *do*'. There is another equally important point. Asking questions can actually *change* things. Let's suppose I ask you to imagine a dog in the park. Now I ask you some questions. Does the dog have a collar? What colour is it? Is it playing with a ball? What colour is the ball? Is the dog wagging its tail? Is it sniffing the ground? In all probability, each question will change the image you first created in your mind.

Modelling is the way infants acquire knowledge and skills. They observe – the implicit phase. Then they try things out for themselves. What works they keep, what doesn't work they reject – the explicit phase. For learning Erickson's hypnotherapy skills, this two-stage modelling process was perfect. Let's begin by looking at the way it functions in such an ideal situation. Then we'll see how it can be adapted for different kinds of uses in everyday life.

The implicit modelling phase

I'm typing these words with only an occasional glance at the keyboard. And yet, if you ask me to tell you where each individual letter is *I haven't the slightest idea.* In other words, my conscious mind doesn't know, but my unconscious mind does and it directs my fingers accordingly.

It's just a simple illustration of the fact that when it comes to many accomplishments – but especially to physical skills – people don't always know themselves what they do. It would be useless asking me questions. It's also an illustration of the fact that it's almost always the unconscious mind that knows best in these kinds of situations. Once you've learned to do something, such that it becomes automatic:

Conscious analysis actually inhibits performance.

When I started snowboarding I, like most beginners, was scared of turning across the slope. Analysing the turn consciously, I saw that halfway through the manoeuvre my snowboard would be pointing straight down the mountain. It seemed I would inevitably accelerate out of control. And the more I thought about it, the more nervous I became.

Of course, eventually, like everyone else, I did learn how to make turns. It simply required the belief. I saw other people doing it and accepted that it must be possible. In other words, I stopped trying to analyse the turn consciously and, instead, gave the problem over to my unconscious mind.

But the most fascinating thing is this: if I ever do attempt to control a turn consciously – because, for example, the slope is unusually steep – then the nerves return and *I can't do it.*

That's not really surprising. Because in order to turn my snowboard consciously, I would have to compute quite a lot of things.

For example, I would have to calculate how far I have to lean with respect to the slope, the radius of the turn and the speed that I expect to be travelling. In fact, I haven't the slightest idea how to do that. Even if I did, the calculation would take so long that there wouldn't be time to make more than one turn before the lifts closed for the day. And even if I had the answer to that calculation, how would I consciously put my body at an angle of, say, 63 degrees?

At the conscious level this is impossible. But my unconscious mind can not only solve the problem, it can also put my body in precisely the right position. Of course, it doesn't use the same techniques of analysis that my conscious mind would. It's all to do with sensing the forces and making a constant series of small adjustments by trial and error. But it's no less remarkable for that. What it all comes down to is this:

> **You must have faith in your unconscious.**

No matter what the sport or physical activity, the same applies.

If you're not convinced about the futility of asking people about skills that have become automatic, try posing the following questions to any motorist:

- ▶ *If you want to indicate a left turn, do you use a control that's on the left-hand side of the steering wheel or the right-hand side?*
- ▶ *If you want to use the windscreen wipers, do you move a control on the right-hand side of the wheel or the left-hand side?*
- ▶ *If you're stopped at traffic lights, will you next see them go from red to orange to green or will they go directly from red to green?*
- ▶ *If you see brake lights on a car about eight vehicles ahead of you, do you take your foot off the accelerator or do you wait until you see the brake lights on the vehicle in front?*
- ▶ *If you have a manual gear stick, at what speed do you change from first to second? How many revolutions per minute is that?*

They'll probably not be able to answer any of those points very confidently. The big question, then, is this. How best can you uncover the information contained in someone else's unconscious mind and transfer it to your unconscious mind, so you can do the same things?

NLP sees conventional learning as divided into four main stages.

- ▶ **Unconscious incompetence:** *at this stage you know nothing.*
- ▶ **Conscious incompetence:** *you've now begun to practise the skill. You're not very good at it, but at least improvement is rapid because you're starting from a low level.*
- ▶ **Conscious competence:** *by this stage you've acquired a good level of skill, but further improvement takes enormous time and effort and everything still requires concentration.*
- ▶ **Unconscious competence:** *you've now arrived at the stage at which you can perform the activity automatically at a high level, without having to think about what you're doing.*

A faster way of learning would be to skip the conscious stages and accomplish the whole process unconsciously – from unconscious to unconscious. But is this possible?

In the 1980s and 90s a group of neurophysiologists at the University of Parma, Italy, made an important discovery about the process of learning. Working with macaque monkeys, they detected neurons that fired not only when the monkeys carried out a particular action but also when they *saw* another monkey, or person, perform that action.

Obviously we all already knew that we and many other animals could copy. Nothing very startling about that. But if you stop and think about those neurons for a moment you'll realize how extremely significant a breakthrough it was. It means – for macaque monkeys, at least – that seeing an action carried out creates the same 'experience' in that part of the mind *as actually doing it*.

Think of pounding a nail into a board - muscle neurons "fire"!

Such neurons have been dubbed 'mirror neurons' because they allow actions to be mirrored. If they're proven to exist in humans (and not all scientists have accepted that) then they provide an explanation of implicit modelling.

HAVE A GO

Step 1: Find your model. Ideally, this is the world's greatest expert. Your model also needs to be relevant to your particular circumstances. For example, if at the age of 40 you want to start your own business from scratch, you won't get the answers you need by modelling a successful businessman who inherited his company from his father. If you'd like to play the guitar but have a finger missing, then you need to find a great guitarist who also has a finger missing. And so on. Your model also has to be someone you can observe in depth for a sufficient period of time. That's easy in some disciplines, much harder in others.

Step 2: Prepare for each modelling session by getting yourself in a heightened state of awareness. The point, of course, is to make it possible to absorb information you might not otherwise have noticed, either consciously or unconsciously. For that reason, Milton Erickson would sometimes put himself into a trance to make himself more sensitive to his patients. You could try the Betty Erickson self-hypnosis method described in Chapter 1 – when required to state the purpose you say something like: 'I am entering into a state of self-hypnosis so that I can hand over to my unconscious mind the task of absorbing the techniques used by my model.' You could also try the 'flow' technique described below.

Step 3: Observe your model in action. Do *not* make any attempt to describe what's going on, either by writing it down, or describing it out loud, or even by thinking it in words. Nor should you ask any questions. Simply try to absorb.

Step 4: As soon as you feel able, try copying your model. Continue observing and copying until you can do the same things.

The explicit modelling phase

At the end of the implicit phase you can reproduce the same results as your chosen expert. That, anyway, would be the case in an ideal modelling situation. But you still don't necessarily know *how* you're doing it. In the explicit modelling phase you therefore use 'subtraction'. That's to say, you leave something out and see what happens.

Let's say you had been modelling Milton Erickson and you had noticed that at a certain point he began breathing very audibly and very slowly. Is that something that contributed to the hypnotic effect? Having precisely copied everything Milton Erickson did, and having obtained the same results that he obtained, you would, on another occasion, omit the slow, audible breathing and see what happened. If you still got the original result you would know the breathing was superfluous. Conversely, if your technique was no longer successful, you would know the breathing was crucial.

Clearly, the explicit phase can be laborious and time-consuming. There could be hundreds of things to check. You may well conclude that, for your purposes, it's enough to be able to get the results you want, even if some of the things you're doing are irrelevant. On the other hand, if you want to be a world-beater that's the kind of attention to detail that's essential.

Bandler and Grinder were quite unabashed if their modelling seemed to be contradicted by scientific studies or statistics. The test for them was that the model worked and the proof of that would be that they could systematically achieve the same results as the person they were modelling. An even stronger test would be to teach the model to a third person and see if that person could also achieve the same results.

As they explained it in *Frogs Into Princes*: 'We have no idea about the "real" nature of things, and we're not particularly interested in what's "true". The function of modelling is to arrive at descriptions which are *useful*.'

WHEN TO USE MODELLING

When it came to the techniques used by Milton Erickson and other therapists, NLP modelling worked perfectly because two conditions were met:

1 *Everything the therapists did was transparent – Bandler and Grinder could see and hear all that went on.*
2 *The skills used by the therapists could (more or less) be reproduced by anyone.*

But that isn't always the case. Suppose John Grinder were to come to model me as I write (of the two men, he's the one now most dedicated to modelling). He would watch me sitting at my computer typing silently away, with very little insight into my thought processes. He wouldn't hear me speak except to curse myself now and then for some stupid error. He'd see me refer to reference books or seek information online. He'd see me break off to make myself a cup of tea or check weather reports to see if I might go snowboarding or swimming or whatever it might be. I don't think he'd learn very much. So modelling won't work for everything.

> **Modelling is an additional learning skill, to be added to your existing repertoire.**

Consider, for example:

▶ *a mentalist who has the ability to remember extremely long numbers*
▶ *an expert skier demonstrating deep powder technique*
▶ *a world-class cellist.*

In the first example, no matter how long your implicit modelling phase, you will never absorb any ability at memorizing numbers because everything goes on inside the brain. The whole process is invisible. In the second example, you could certainly absorb some of the technique through implicit modelling, but a highly significant part of what the powder expert does is hidden from view beneath the snow. Moreover, even if you could learn the skills by implicit modelling you would still have to find a way of acquiring the confidence to apply them (see Chapter 5). And as regards a world-class cellist, no one beginning to study music as an adult could ever reproduce the same sounds through modelling or, indeed, any other technique yet devised.

So NLP modelling has its limitations and has to be applied creatively according to the kind of skill being studied.

There is another point. If you want to learn to be an Ericksonian hypnotherapist today the answer is to model the best among his successors. Right? Wrong! That work has already been done. The special Ericksonian skills Bandler and Grinder identified were recorded by them, published (see Chapter 11) and can now be learned by students all over the world, including you if you wish. The only point in modelling a hypnotherapist today would be if that person had moved the whole science forward and was achieving results that no one had achieved before.

And the same applies to many other fields. If you want to learn the special habits of various kinds of geniuses, all you have to do is read books by those who have applied the NLP modelling methods to them.

If it turns out to be the case that the techniques employed by the experts in your chosen field have *not* been modelled, are you ever going to get access to those people and are you going to have the time? Probably not.

For most of us, then, it's a question of extracting what we can in practical terms from a limited version of the modelling technique. Here are some suggestions:

▶ *If you can model exceptional people, so much the better. There was, in fact, a huge difference between the results achieved by Erickson and those achieved by other hypnotherapists using what appeared to be similar methods. He was curing people, often very rapidly, where some other hypnotherapists were failing utterly. So, as it turned out, it was crucial to discover what Erickson was doing that was different. But, on the other hand, for the purposes of you learning how to do something like play golf or swim, it's not actually essential to model the world's greatest expert – someone who is thoroughly competent will normally suffice.*

▶ *The easiest way of pinning an expert down is usually to pay for lessons. Choose someone who understands implicit modelling and is amenable to you following that approach. Another possibility would be to get a job working for the model.*

▶ *Don't just watch your model from first position – also try to become the person you're modelling, seeing what they're seeing and feeling what they're feeling from second position. (If you've forgotten about multiple perspectives, turn back to Chapter 2.)*

▶ *You can effectively extend the observation period by making your own videos and playing them back again and again... and again. Professionally made DVDs will probably never show all the things you need, unless the film makers are experienced modellers, but in the absence of a flesh-and-blood expert they're better than nothing and, like your own videos, you can watch them over and over. You may also find clips of useful models on websites such as YouTube. As well as watching at normal speed, use slow motion and freeze-frame.*

▶ *You may think you're faithfully copying your expert, but can you be sure? Have someone film you.*

▶ *Some people dress like their models, take on their mannerisms and habits, and learn to speak like them. It might sound extreme, even a little crazy, but it can be effective. In the first place, it's a kind of self-hypnosis. The more you look like someone, the more you feel like someone, the more you act like someone. Secondly, it's difficult to know what aspects of your model's behaviour contribute to success. The more comprehensively you copy – and the less you exclude – the better your chance of reproducing what your model can do.*

In *Frogs Into Princes*, Bandler and Grinder conceded that 'nothing NLP can accomplish is new'. What was new, they claimed, was the way NLP made learning easier, more productive and more exciting. 'We are on the threshold,' they wrote, 'of a quantum jump in human experience and capability'.

Belief

In order to be able to do something you have to believe you can do it. When it comes to anything new, you have to believe both that you have the ability to learn and the ability to do that new thing.

If you doubt your ability to learn, you won't learn. It's just about as simple as that. When he needed patients to learn something new and difficult, Milton Erickson would often get them to think of the way they learned to walk, to talk, to read and so on. Here's a visualization to remind you how enormous your learning ability truly is.

HAVE A GO
Step 1: Close your eyes, travel back in time and imagine yourself as an infant. See yourself crawling about on the floor. Think of how enormous everything seems, how impossibly huge. Really enter into the experience. Look up at the table towering above you. Take hold of the leg and haul yourself up. You're standing upright for the very first time in your life. You did it! And now everything else looks just that little bit more manageable.

Step 2: Think of the sound of voices as you lie in your cot. They're no more meaningful than the noises made by people speaking, say, Russian or Chinese today. You can't even tell where one noise ends and another noise begins. But you're persistent. Day after day you listen and gradually you learn to recognize patterns and isolate one noise from another. Day after day you try to copy the sounds. And one day you say, 'Dada'. You've just spoken your very first word.

Step 3: See yourself at school. You're very tiny. Your feet don't even touch the floor as you sit at the table. A book is open in front of you. There's a big colour picture and underneath it some black marks. You put your finger by the black marks and, slowly and laboriously, you spell out 'd... o... g'. You've just read your very first word.

Step 4: Now think about whatever it is you wish to learn today. How difficult can it be compared with all that you already achieved as an infant? Not very difficult at all.

ACHIEVING 'FLOW' OR 'THE ZONE'

Have there ever been times in your life when, to your own surprise, you rose to a challenge with ease? When you accomplished things you never thought you could? I'm sure there have. It happens to everyone now and then – especially in the physical realm. Sports people call it 'flow' or 'being in the zone'. When a tennis player is in the zone, every ball lands one millimetre inside the line instead of one millimetre outside. Unfortunately, for most of us, it's a rare experience.

When you're modelling, or when you're learning by any method, it helps to get into a state of flow. Flow seems to occur when the level of challenge is high enough to create an usual degree of focus (especially when both mental and physical skills are involved) but not high enough to create negative stress. Using this principle, there are ways of creating flow artificially.

HAVE A GO
Step 1: Prepare a chart of the first 25 letters of the alphabet written in five rows of five letters, large enough to be read at a distance of a metre or so. Under each letter write, at random, either 'l' (for left), 'r' (for right) or 't' (for together).

Step 2: Pin the chart to a wall at eye level.

Step 3: Begin the game by calling out the letters of the alphabet in turn from 'a' to 'y' and, at the same time, as indicated, raising your left arm (l), your right arm (r) or both together (t). Continue for two minutes.

Step 4: Repeat Step 3, but running backwards through the alphabet from 'y' to 'a'. Continue for two minutes.

Step 5: Finally, spend ten minutes running through from 'y' to 'a' but this time simultaneously raising the left leg with the right arm, the right leg with the left arm and, at the instruction 't', jumping with both legs and swinging both arms. It's essential that the movements are made rhythmically, with the minimum of effort and the maximum grace and, ideally, there should be someone acting as a 'coach' to make sure that is so.

Hopefully, you'll now be in a state of mind that could be described as flow. In that state of mind you should be able to model, and learn, and act at a higher level than normal.

SELF-HYPNOSIS FOR LEARNING

The Betty Erickson self-hypnosis method can also be used to help you learn. If you've forgotten how to put yourself into a trance, refer back to Chapter 1. When you're stating the purpose of your self-hypnosis (Step 3) say something like: 'I am entering into a trance for the purpose of allowing my unconscious mind to make the adjustments that will help me absorb information quickly, easily and without resistance, and to recall it whenever I wish.' Alternatively you could state the specific subject you wish to learn: 'I am entering into a trance for the purpose of allowing my unconscious mind to make the adjustments that will help me learn French/ride a horse/play the violin (or whatever it might be). When you come to the visualization (Steps 5f and 5g), imagine a scene in which you are successfully learning to do whatever you wish.

10 THINGS TO REMEMBER

1   *Your learning ability is the key to almost everything in life.*

2   *If one person can do something, anyone can learn to do it.*

3   *Modelling is all about discovering the things experts and geniuses do 'without knowing about them'.*

4   *Implicit modelling means unconsciously absorbing what someone else does, without asking questions and without applying verbal descriptions.*

5   *Explicit modelling means consciously deducing which of the expert's actions you've now absorbed are important and which are irrelevant.*

6   *Once you've learned to do something, such that it becomes automatic, conscious analysis actually inhibits performance.*

7   *The ideal way of learning would be from an expert's unconscious directly to your unconscious.*

8   *Don't just watch your model from a dissociated position but also try to become the person you're modelling.*

9   *Your learning ability is enormous – believe in it.*

10 *You can improve your modelling ability and your learning skills by inducing a state of flow.*

HOW AM I GETTING ON?

▶ *Are you open to new learning experiences?*

▶ *Have you resolved to learn some new skills?*

▶ *Do you believe that if one person can do something, you too can learn to do it?*

▶ *Have you found a model or models?*

▶ *Have you been able to put yourself into the state of flow that will make modelling more insightful?*

▶ *Have you actually modelled anyone?*

▶ *Have you tried making a video of your model or models?*

▶ *Have you been able to increase your belief in your learning ability?*

▶ *Have you tried self-hypnosis as a way of improving your learning ability?*

It obviously takes a while to set up modelling sessions, so I wouldn't expect you to have done it yet. But you could certainly be practising the skills on a friend straight away. And you could certainly be developing an open and positive learning mindset. So if you haven't been able to answer 'Yes' to at least five questions, read the chapter again, and at least make a start on modelling.

4

....

Transform your inner voice

In this chapter you will learn:
- *how to silence a negative inner voice*
- *how to Swish doubts away*
- *how to reframe things more positively*
- *how to hold a dialogue with your unconscious.*

There's no such thing as failure, only feedback.

NLP presupposition

What are you doing today that makes you feel nervous? Maybe you're going to the bank to ask for a loan. Maybe you have a job interview. Maybe it's a horse riding lesson.

And it doesn't help that someone is telling you, 'You're not going to be able to pull this off.'

Who on earth would say a thing like that?

In fact, it's the same person who for years has been telling you you're not attractive, not witty, not smart, and generally not much good at anything.

And that person is... *you.*

Or rather, as it seems, a person who lives inside of you, almost as someone quite separate.

We all have an inner voice. Or even several different ones.
The problem is that most people's inner voices are unrelentingly
negative. They tend to say things like, 'What's the matter with you?
You really made a mess of that... *again*. Can't you do anything
right?' And so on.

> **Insight**
>
> What do you answer when someone greets you and asks
> 'How are you?' Most people reply with a negative: 'Can't
> complain'; 'Mustn't grumble'; 'Not so bad'. It's such a
> common way of thinking that most of us don't even notice.
> Next time someone asks you, say something positive and see
> what effect it has on both of you: 'Fantastic!'; 'Wonderful!';
> 'It's great to be alive!'

If you have a negative inner voice, then it's in for a little bit of a
shock. Richard Bandler recounts that he often tells his to 'Shut the
f*** up!'

If yours is saying anything negative, do the same – right now. It
helps, sometimes quite a lot. But NLP also has a few rather more
sophisticated techniques.

Discrediting an inner voice

Rather than simply trying to shout louder than your inner voice,
a more effective method is to *discredit* it. Inner voices are
convincing but they aren't necessarily any more right than any
other voices.

One way *not* to believe it is to *change* the voice. Right now it
probably sounds authoritative. But what if it were to sound like
the voice of the politician you most distrust? Then maybe you
wouldn't take such notice of it.

HAVE A GO

Step 1: Think of a person you greatly distrust. It could be someone you know, it could be a contemporary politician or it could be a historical figure such as Hitler. Hear their voice and identify what qualities (submodalities) in the voice make you distrustful. Is there something about the pitch, perhaps? The rhythm? The timbre?

Step 2: Now think of the negative thing your inner voice has been telling you, but instead of hearing the usual voice, hear instead the distrusted voice, complete with all those unreliable, cheating, lying submodalities. Really enter into this experience. See the face of that distrusted person and realize that you don't believe a word they're saying. It may be helpful to play some music in your head, perhaps something that comes from a satirical programme or which somehow symbolizes indomitable opposition (if you're familiar with it, the Colonel Bogey March works well).

Step 3: Now push that distrusted voice and its distrusted, negative message further and further away from you until it gets fainter and fainter and you can't hear it any more.

Step 4: Check to see how you now feel – hopefully a lot less negative.

Step 5: Future pace (see below) by visualizing yourself successfully doing the very thing your negative voice had been telling you that you couldn't do.

Step 6: Actually *do* the thing your negative voice had been telling you that you couldn't do.

Jargon buster – future pacing

Future pacing simply means visualizing a scene in the future in which you behave in the way you want. That will help you install the new behaviour in your unconscious.

Swish your doubts away

Sometimes it's more a case of being overwhelmed by a general *feeling* of doubt than by specific criticisms. A special visualization known as the Swish can help.

HAVE A GO

Step 1: Think of some quality or ability in yourself about which you have doubts that you'd like to sweep away. Do you have doubts about your attractiveness, for example, or about your physical coordination, or your persuasiveness? Call up an image associated with those doubts (Image 1). For example, you might have doubts about your ability to make a speech. In that case you might see yourself waiting to go to the podium. Now identify the submodalities that are associated with doubt. Do you, perhaps, get a fluttering feeling in your stomach? Is the visualization blurry? Is the image in a particular position?

Step 2: Clear that visualization away by saying your telephone number backwards.

Step 3: Now think of some positive quality in yourself about which you have no doubts at all, about which you feel only certainty. How about your love for your children? Or your dog? Or your home town? Call up an image that exemplifies that certainty (Image 2). Now identify the submodalities associated with certainty. Perhaps you feel something rising up in your chest that makes you want to punch the air? Is the visualization clear? Is it, perhaps, very colourful?

Step 4: Fully experience certainty and the image associated with certainty (Image 2) and then, suddenly, Swish (that's to say, swap) that image, and only the image, for the image about which you have doubts (Image 1). It's essential that you maintain the submodalities associated with certainty – and all the feelings associated with certainty – and that you attach them to Image 1, so you see yourself succeeding.

Step 5: You should now begin to feel about Image 1 the same way you felt about Image 2. That's to say, certainty about your ability to succeed. Repeat the process several times straight off. Then go out and test the result by doing the very thing about which you previously doubted yourself.

Step 6: Continue to alternate the visualization exercise and the practical test until your doubts are gone.

Insight

In NLP this exercise is more commonly done in reverse, attaching doubts to negative evaluations about yourself, rather than attaching certainty to positive evaluations. In my experience, it's much easier to do it the way I've described.

Reframing the negative

We first met reframing in Chapter 2. If you've forgotten about it, turn back and refresh your memory. Essentially, reframing means changing the context in which you think about something. By so doing, you can completely change your attitude to that thing, so that you feel better about it or think of yourself more positively.

Whenever you notice your inner voice using a negative frame, you should question it and see if a positive frame doesn't fit better.

Here's an exercise for reframing an inner voice that can also be a lot of fun.

Step 1: Think of a situation about which your inner voice has been saying negative things. It could be something from the past or it could be something you're going to be doing in the future.

Step 2: Freeze-frame the single moment from your internal movie that most encapsulates that negativity.

Step 3: Now try playing around with the image. If there are people who intimidate you, why not cut them down to size? Literally – make them little. Why not give them some accessories? Maybe funny hats and red noses. How do you see yourself? Why not portray yourself like a hero or an Amazon from a classical painting? When you're satisfied with the revised image, experiment with different colours, textures, backgrounds and so on. For example, you could make it into a cartoon, a photo-realistic oil painting or maybe a moody watercolour. Once you've discovered the style that most helps you to feel the way you'd like to feel, fix it in your mind.

Step 4: Select a frame for your modified image. You don't have to use an oblong or square frame – it could equally be round or oval. It doesn't have to be gilt – it could be natural wood, coloured plastic, stainless steel or anything else you want. Again, the idea is to choose a frame that's the most compatible with the way you want to feel. As a finishing touch, add a picture light.

Step 5: Stand back and look at the new image in its new frame. You should now feel much more as you'd like to feel. If not, try manipulating the image and the frame again.

Insight
When my inner voice knew how many thousands of people were ahead of me at the end of my first marathon it wasn't very pleased: 'You should have done better than that,' it said.

So I got the figures for my specific age group – that made things look better. And then I pointed out to my inner voice that, what's more, most of those in my age group had run marathons before. By reframing in this way I was able to enjoy pride in my first attempt rather than disappointment.

REFRAMING GOALS

In Chapter 7 we'll learn about the perils of framing instructions to other people in negative terms. The same equally applies to your inner voice when it gives instructions to you. For example, it's quite pointless for your inner voice to tell you 'Don't think too much about getting hurt', because then you *immediately* think about getting hurt. It's the same as if someone tells you, 'Don't think of pink giraffes'. You immediately have to think of pink giraffes. It's impossible not to.

Goals, too, must always be framed in positive terms, never in negative terms. For example, your inner voice should never say something like, 'Don't be so clumsy in the future'. Instead, it should be saying something along the lines of, 'Every day you're becoming more agile, poised and precise in your movements'.

So how can you get your inner voice to reframe things in the way you'd like? One way is simply to correct it every time it's unnecessarily negative.

HAVE A GO
All this week, be alert to negatives from your inner voice and as soon as they crop up, reframe them in a positive way.

Using multiple perspectives

Changing perspectives is a useful technique whenever your negative inner voice is really laying it on thick. And especially when it's providing frightening images to discourage you. 'Look at this,' it says.

'This is how you're going to look after you've crashed/fallen over/ made an idiot of yourself in front of all those people.'

We first encountered multiple perspectives in Chapter 2. The one we want here is third position or dissociation. In other words, we're going to minimize the emotional impact by adopting the position of an outsider.

HAVE A GO
For example, let's say that you're at the top of a steep ski slope – a black run. You want to do it but you're apprehensive. From the bottom it hadn't looked so bad but now you're up here it looks horribly dangerous. The answer in this case is to switch to the perspective of someone at the bottom of the run looking up and seeing you. In other words, you dissociate from your predicament. Now it doesn't seem so steep, does it? Watch yourself coming down – and make it good.

NARROW CAMERA ANGLE

Narrow camera angle is a variation on multiple perspectives that I use quite a lot in intimidating physical situations. It's basically an elaboration of the traditional advice given to people scared of heights: 'Don't look down'. You remain associated (that's to say, in first position) but you limit your field of view, both via your eyes *and in your imagination* to things that are familiar and harmless. It also works with things like visits to the dentist.

Insight
A friend invited me to try canyoning in the Pyrenees, a sport in which he is something of an expert. It means descending a limestone mountain via a riverbed. Rivers have a way of getting down mountains by the fastest route, so there were lots of vertical descents which required either leaping into rock pools way below, or abseiling. I focused on nothing other than the moves I had to make. Every time my inner voice said, 'Look how high these waterfalls are' so I'd reply, 'I'm far too busy fastening this rope'. I didn't allow myself to

think of the rocks below, the possibility of the pitons pulling out, or the rope breaking, nothing. I barely noticed the scenery, and I did it – all due to 'narrow camera angle'.

Questioning an inner voice

So far we've learned to shut out, ignore and overwrite negativity and doubt. What we're going to do next is analyse what the negative inner voice is saying and uncover the holes in its arguments.

According to Bandler and Grinder, much of the success achieved by the therapists Fritz Perls and Virginia Satir was due to this very process of confronting their clients' inner voices.

'Magic is hidden in the language we speak,' Bandler and Grinder wrote in *The Structure of Magic*. 'The webs that you can tie and untie are at your command if only you pay attention to… the incantations…'.

The incantations we're interested in here are known as 'challenges'. Bandler and Grinder reduced all the varied things that Perls and Satir said to just a dozen or so different kinds of challenges. They called them the Meta Model, because both Perls and Satir had 'a map or model for changing their clients' models'.

The Meta Model, then, was originally devised to help professional therapists achieve the same results for their clients that Perls and Satir did. But you can equally use it to challenge yourself and your own models of the world.

According to the Meta Model, your 'internal map' has defects caused by:

▶ *generalization*
▶ *deletion*
▶ *distortion.*

Once you become aware of those defects, so you can transform your inner voice.

Generalization

Generalization, according to *The Structure of Magic*, is the process by which elements of a person's model 'become detached from their original experience and come to represent the entire category of which the experience is an example'. If as a child you were burned by a saucepan, you might have learned to be careful of *all* hot things, not just saucepans. That's useful. But suppose you had been bitten by *one* dog and thereafter avoided *all* dogs. In that case, the generalization would have unnecessarily limited your choices and your opportunities for enjoyment.

Deletion

Deletion is the process by which we all pay attention to *some* aspects of the data we're receiving via our senses but not others. There's a good reason for this. We'd be overloaded by information if we didn't edit it in some way. But once again it means that our maps of the world are quite different from the actual territory. Bandler and Grinder give the example of a man who complained his wife never said anything caring to him. But when they visited him at home they heard his wife say caring things. When this was pointed out the man would say that he hadn't heard – he was literally deleting the things she was saying.

Distortion

In an experiment people were *quickly* shown various playing cards one at a time and asked to identify them. Most of the cards were normal but a few had been altered so that, for example, the six of spades was red and the four of hearts was black. No one noticed anything strange – the subjects were distorting what they were seeing to make it fit in with their *existing* models.

Some degree of generalization, deletion and distortion, therefore, is both necessary and inevitable if we're to be able to think effectively and to express ourselves to others. Problems arise when these processes become too extreme and especially too negative.

NLP subdivides these three categories into around a dozen or so specific kinds of 'violation'. Some of these have rather weird titles, deriving from Grinder's background in linguistics, for example: 'lost performatives', 'nominalizations' and 'lack of referential index'. This makes the whole subject sound a lot more complicated than it really is.

HAVE A GO
In effect, Perls and Satir would bring about change simply by asking questions whenever they encountered damaging examples of generalization, deletion or distortion. For example, if a client said 'everyone' was against them the question might be, 'Everyone?' In that deceptively simple way, the client would be forced to acknowledge the generalization and look at things differently.

Below I've given some examples of the negative kinds of things your inner voice might sometimes say to you. Take a look at them and decide whether they're generalizations, deletions or distortions. Then formulate your challenges.

1 *You're no good at anything.*
2 *You always get it wrong.*
3 *You have a lot of fear.*
4 *You know what she thinks of you.*
5 *His behaviour has driven you to alcohol.*
6 *You're very good at your job.*
7 *You should go to the dinner party.*
8 *It's because he doesn't care about you that he does these things.*

9   *It will be better if you leave.*
10 *You can achieve anything you want.*

———————————————xxx———————————————

So let's see how you got on. Did you notice which were generalizations, which were deletions and which were distortions?

1   *This is a pretty obvious generalization. You might challenge it by saying something like this: 'No good at anything? You mean there's nothing I can do to a reasonable standard? Come on, you know I'm good at…'.*

2   *This is another generalization. Your challenge might be: 'I always get it wrong? You mean I've never once been right? Come on, what about…'.*

3   *This one is a bit more tricky. It's a type of distortion called a 'nominalization' which technically means that a verb has been turned into a noun. In effect, something that's temporary and changeable (being scared) becomes something that appears to be fixed (having fear). The idea of the challenge is to re-establish the temporary nature of the condition: 'What is it that's frightening me?'*

4   *This is an example of another kind of distortion known as 'mind reading'. Your challenge could be: 'How could I possibly know what she thinks?'*

5   *Here two things get linked in a way that is made to seem inevitable – a cause and an effect. But in fact, a distortion is taking place. Your challenge could be: 'How has his behaviour given me no option other than alcohol?'*

6   *I slipped this is in to make sure you're paying attention. It's not negative at all. In fact, it's exactly the kind of thing your inner voice should be saying.*

7   *This is a type of generalization known as a modal operator. A sense of obligation or inevitability is created when none, in fact, exists. Your challenge might be: 'Why should I? What would happen if I didn't go?'*

8   *This generalization is a kind of presupposition. Your inner voice makes sense of something by presupposing something else.*

But it could easily be wrong. The challenge might be: 'How do you know he doesn't care about me?'

9 *This is an example of a comparative deletion. Your inner voice doesn't specify what the action of leaving would be better than – and may not have thought it through. Your challenge might be: 'Better than what? What's the alternative?'*

10 *It might be a generalization but it's not a negative one, so you shouldn't be challenging this at all.*

I've specified some of the sub-categories of Meta Model 'violation' but they're really not significant for our purposes. It's far more important to recognize the negative mindset and to question it every time. When you live with negative generalizations, deletions and distortions every day they can become such a part of your internal landscape that you no longer even notice them. That's a very dangerous situation to get into.

Insight

Obviously some kinds of negative thoughts are essential, otherwise we'd very soon do things that result in injury and even death. What we're concerned with here are thoughts that undermine our abilities and restrain our progress: 'I'd never be able to do that'; 'That's too hard for me'; 'I'll never be any good' and so on. As an experiment, I once made a note every time I had a negative thought during the day. Try it – just mark a dot on a piece of paper or on the back of your hand. You'll probably be astonished by how many dots you accumulate.

Turning your inner voice into a constructive partner

Once you've successfully challenged a negative inner voice, the next step is to get a constructive dialogue going.

A good starting point is the NLP presupposition:

Underlying every behaviour is a positive intention.

In other words, when your inner voice tells you you're useless, it's doing it for a good reason. You need to find out that reason. How? Simply by starting a conversation, like this:

You: 'Why do you keep criticizing me?'

Inner voice: 'Because I want you to sharpen up and pay attention to what you're doing.'

You: 'Well, you're having completely the opposite effect because you're demoralizing me.'

Inner voice: 'So you're weak on top of everything else! Can't take criticism!'

You: 'I'm telling you, if you don't improve I'm getting rid of you.'

Inner voice: 'You wish! Listen, you've got to stop making stupid mistakes.'

You: 'So tell me how. Be more constructive.'

Inner voice: 'All right. You need more patience. Be willing to spend a little more time on preparation before you rush into things. Then you'll be fine.'

You: 'Why couldn't you have put it like that to begin with?'

Did you find that conversation comical or even absurd? If so, you're going to find Six Step Reframing something of a revelation, because you'll be talking to your unconscious in just this way as if it's a separate person. Developed by John Grinder, it's a technique that can be used to change all kinds of behaviour. In this example, we're using it to change the negativity of your unconscious as regards, let's say, any potentially dangerous physical activity. At first Six Step Reframing may well strike you as a little wacky. However, once you try it you'll fairly soon get used to the idea.

Step 1: Identify the behaviour to be changed – in this example, it's the negativity of your unconscious.

Step 2: Get your unconscious to communicate via a reliable involuntary signal. Grinder suggests asking something like: 'Will you, my unconscious, communicate with me?' You must then wait passively with your attention focused on your body for a signal from your unconscious. If you receive a signal, touch the area of your body where the signal occurred and say 'Thank you'. To check, you then ask: 'If the signal just offered means "Yes", please repeat it.' You now need to validate the signal. Asking your unconscious to remain inactive, you now try to reproduce the signal consciously. If you can, then the possibility exists that the signal wasn't a genuine signal from the unconscious and you'll need to repeat the process until you have an authentic involuntary signal.

Step 3: Discover the positive intention behind the behaviour to be changed. In this case you could ask your unconscious: 'What is the positive intention behind the negative comments?' Let's assume you get the answer, 'To prevent you doing something in which you might get hurt.'

Step 4: Having discovered the positive intention, you now need to generate a set of alternatives as good as or better than the original behaviour at satisfying that positive intention. Ask your unconscious: 'Develop an alternative range of behaviours – all of which satisfy the positive intention while nevertheless helping me achieve my goal – and from those select up to three for implementation. When you have completed the task, give me a positive signal.'

Step 5: The alternative behaviours should now be apparent to you. For example, your unconscious might agree to drop the negative comments if you a) accept the need to take more lessons, b) agree to practise the basic manoeuvres more thoroughly, c) be willing to wear protective clothing. Get your unconscious to accept responsibility for implementing the new behaviours. For example, you might ask: 'Will you, my unconscious mind, take responsibility for making sure the new behaviours are followed?'

Step 6: Carry out an ecology check (see Chapter 1) by asking your unconscious to make sure that none of the new behaviours will cause a problem for you or for others.

> **Insight**
>
> Examples of the kind of signal your unconscious could give you that you couldn't very easily reproduce consciously (Step 2) include:
>
> ▶ *tingling down the back of your neck or spine*
> ▶ *fluttering or pulsating of a muscle*
> ▶ *a localized hot or tickling sensation*
> ▶ *a localized numbness.*

SELF-HYPNOSIS

The Betty Erickson self-hypnosis method can also be used to help constrain a negative inner voice. If you've forgotten how to put yourself into a trance, refer back to Chapter 1. When you're stating the purpose of your self-hypnosis (Step 3) say something like: 'I am entering into a trance for the purpose of asking my unconscious mind to limit negative comments to those rare occasions when some serious harm might actually result'. When you come to the visualization (Steps 5f and 5g), imagine yourself behaving in the way you want, freed from unnecessary criticism.

It is hoped that you've now mastered the techniques for dealing with an inner voice that's unjustifiably negative. In the following chapter we'll be taking the next step, which is to develop the positive.

10 THINGS TO REMEMBER

1   You can simply tell a negative inner voice: 'Shut the f*** up!'

2   You can discredit an inner voice by making it sound like someone you distrust.

3   Swishing is a technique that can be used to replace doubt with certainty.

4   Reframing is a new way of looking at something, so that a negative can be changed into a positive.

5   Whenever your inner voice says something negative, you should challenge it.

6   Generalization is the process by which we make ourselves believe that one particular experience is representative of all similar experiences.

7   Deletion is the process by which we filter out information to prevent our brains being overloaded.

8   Distortion is the process by which we make things fit into our existing models of the world, rather than change our models to fit the facts.

9   There's always a positive intention behind a negative message from your unconscious.

10 Six Step Reframing can be used to find other ways of satisfying that positive intention.

HOW AM I GETTING ON?

▶ *When someone asked 'How are you?', did you reply 'Fantastic!'?*

▶ *Have you told your inner voice to 'Shut the f*** up' when it's been negative – and did it shut up?*

▶ *Have you successfully discredited a negative inner voice by making it sound like someone you distrust?*

▶ *Have you been able to Swish doubts away?*

▶ *Have you been able to reframe something you saw in a negative light as something you can now see in a positive light?*

▶ *Have you discovered any examples of generalization, deletion and distortion in your thoughts?*

▶ *If so, have you been able to correct them?*

▶ *Have you totalled up how many negative thoughts you have in one day?*

▶ *Have you been able to discover a positive intention behind at least one criticism by your inner voice?*

▶ *If so, have you been able to find a new and more creative way of satisfying that positive intention?*

If you answered 'No' to four or more questions, refer back to the relevant parts of the chapter and have a go at the practical exercises. You simply can't allow that negative inner voice to continue doing damage.

5

Transform your success

In this chapter you will learn:
- *how to program yourself for success*
- *how to increase your motivation*
- *how you can automatically behave exactly as you would wish*
- *how you can reverse engineer your future.*

If what you are doing isn't working, do something else.

NLP presupposition

As Richard Bandler likes to point out, if you're looking for difficulties you'll always find them. Instead, he says, you should be looking to see what *works*. In the last chapter we learned how *not* to look for difficulties. In this chapter we're going to examine the second part of his prescription.

Starting the day

Let's start right at the beginning of the day. What time is that for you? Maybe an austere 6 a.m.? A more relaxed 7.30 a.m.? Or perhaps a thoroughly decadent 9 a.m.? In fact, the day doesn't start when you wake up. A day starts *when you go to bed*. It's what you do *then* that sets the tone for the next 24 hours.

Have you ever had to get up early for something important? Of course you have. And the night before did you say something like: 'I must wake up at 6 a.m., I must wake up at 6 a.m.'? And it worked, didn't it?

Something in people is quite good at measuring time. And priming yourself just before you go to sleep is usually effective because, when you're drifting off, you have good access to your unconscious. Think about it. If it can work with time it can work for other things as well.

So what you do is not only prime yourself to wake up *before* the alarm, but wake up full of optimism. Bandler says he wants people to wake up and ask: 'How much fun can I have today?'; 'How much freedom can I find?'; 'How much more can I do than I've ever done before?' Programming that attitude is done the night before.

All you have to do, when you're drifting off, is say something along these lines: 'I am now going to have a wonderful night's sleep, and when I wake up at 7 a.m. I will feel completely refreshed and full of enthusiasm and optimism for the things I am going to be doing.'

Elaborate on that as you wish. You might like to conjure up images of the marvellous things you're going to be achieving. Have your alarm set for just after 7 a.m. (or whatever time you've chosen) but solely as a back-up. You'll not only find that you wake up on your own *before* the alarm but that you feel positive about the day ahead. So that's a pretty good start.

(Incidentally, if you sleep with someone else don't go leaping out of bed before you've had a nice cuddle – see Chapter 8.)

Getting motivated

Okay. So you're up. You're feeling good. Now you need to motivate yourself for the next big step.

NLP makes a distinction between two different kinds of motivation:

▶ *motivation* away *from something*
▶ *motivation* towards *something.*

Let's suppose you grew up in financially difficult circumstances. You knew what it was like to be hungry, you knew what it was like to be cold and you knew what it was like to wear the same clothes day after day, week after week. Now that you're an adult you have a burning desire to be wealthy because you don't ever want to experience that kind of poverty again. That's motivation *away* from something.

Now let's suppose you're someone who grew up in an affluent family and have a well-paid job. But you still want to achieve more in the material sense. You dream of ocean-going yachts, private planes, heli-skiing in the winter, the Mediterranean in summer and so on. That's motivation *towards* something.

Of course, motivation direction doesn't have to be concerned with money. You can be motivated *away* from discomfort, confrontation, criticism, fear, pain, embarrassment, failure and so on, just as you can be motivated *towards* comfort, tranquillity, praise, success and much more.

Nobody is wholly 'away from' or 'towards' but – for any given type of situation – we all have a tendency to be mostly one or the other. In order to motivate yourself effectively, it helps to understand your own personality in this respect.

HAVE A GO
Think about the following and ask yourself whether your motivation is more 'away from' or more 'towards':

▶ *studying*
▶ *going to work*
▶ *watching television*

- ▶ *meeting friends*
- ▶ *reading*
- ▶ *making love.*

STOKING UP MOTIVATION

Having decided what kind of motivation works best with you, you can then stoke it up.

Suppose that, for various reasons, you wish to give up something – for example, gambling. You've tried and you've failed. And the reason is this. You're motivated to stop gambling but your motivation to continue gambling is even stronger. Let's suppose you're an 'away from' person. What you have to do is stoke up your motivation *not* to gamble, until it overwhelms your motivation *to* gamble. In other words, to get you to the point at which you say 'enough is enough'. This is how to bring on that feeling through visualization.

HAVE A GO

Step 1: Think of five negative scenes connected with gambling (or whatever it might be). You could, for example, visualize the arrival of household bills you can't pay because you've lost money. You might think of how upset your partner is. You might think of the toll the stress is taking on your health. And so on.

Step 2: Run the five scenes in your mind one after the other to make your own 'anti-gambling' film. Then run them all again but faster. Then again, faster still. Continue until you have the overwhelming feeling 'enough is enough'.

Insight

If you're a 'towards' person you would use the same procedure but stacking five images of how wonderful it is to be a non-gambler.

Borrowing motivation

We all have things we need to do for which we can't get any motivation at all, either 'away from' or 'towards'.

NLP can help by, as it were, letting you borrow motivation from something you *do* enjoy. The following visualization utilizes the Swish technique which you're now familiar with.

HAVE A GO

Step 1: Think of something you enjoy immensely and for which you feel tremendous motivation – for example, a romantic evening with your lover (Image 1). Make a note of the submodalities associated with that motivational drive.

Step 2: Think of the thing you've got to do but for which you feel no motivation – for example, housework (Image 2).

Step 3: Revel in Image 1. See, feel, touch, taste and smell everything associated with it. Spin it up as much as possible. Just when everything is at a peak, suddenly Swish Image 2 into the position occupied by Image 1. Maintain the submodalities from Image 1. Revel in your new, highly motivated attitude to this thing for which you previously felt no motivation at all. Repeat the Swish several times until you just can't wait to start on Image 2 for real.

Step 4: Go and do it.

Insight

You may be able to bolster your motivation further by thinking of ways that dealing with one thing could actually *lead* to the other. For example, getting the housework done and the bedroom clean and tidy (Image 2) might really lead to a romantic evening (Image 1).

The Circle of Confidence

So you're up. And you're motivated. But you still need something more. You need the belief that you can succeed. You need confidence.

If you hadn't had confidence when you were an infant, you never would have learned to stand up, to walk, to talk, to feed yourself, to read or acquire all the other skills you have. As an infant the concept of 'failure' had no meaning for you. You just kept on plugging away until you succeeded.

Unfortunately, as we get older, the word 'failure' begins to fill us with terror. We reach a point where we'd rather not try than fail. We reason that if we haven't tried we haven't failed. And that seems to be easier to live with.

Well, this is one case in which an 'infantile' attitude is best.

The Circle of Confidence is a technique for transferring confidence from a situation in which you feel mastery to a situation in which you feel inadequate. Some people climb mountains or sail round the world single-handed to try to convince themselves that they can have the self-confidence to tackle just about any situation. They theorize that if they take on the world's hardest challenges, then nothing else will ever seem difficult again. But life isn't quite like that.

NLP does things differently. It allows you to take the self-confidence you felt in any previous situation, including one that was *easy*, and then it transfers that feeling to the more difficult situation.

HAVE A GO
This is my variation on the Circle of Confidence, which I've found works well.

Step 1: Something important is coming up. Think of a quality you'll need if you're going to handle that situation to the best of your abilities. In this example we're focusing on confidence, but you could also use the procedure for other qualities.

Step 2: Search your memory for a past situation in which you felt that necessary confidence. It doesn't have to have been an especially difficult situation. Relive that confident time, seeing and hearing everything in as much detail as possible. Particularly notice how you looked and how the confidence was oozing out of you.

Step 3: Imagine a circle on the floor. Take the confidence you feel and pour it into the circle. Immediately the circle takes on a colour – the colour that, to you, is the colour of confidence. It also makes a noise. Maybe it's a buzzing sound or even music – again, it's whatever expresses confidence to you.

Step 4: Are there any other qualities you'll need? Maybe patience? Maybe judgement? If so, repeat the procedure, also pouring those qualities into your circle.

Step 5: Turn your thoughts to the future occasion when you'll want to feel those qualities. Select a cue to that moment. For example, if you're going to give a speech, the cue could be someone introducing you. Or, if you're going to an interview, it could be a secretary calling your name. (But don't make it too specific otherwise you might never get the cue you envisaged.)

Step 6: Holding that cue in your mind, step into the circle and visualize all those qualities rising up from the floor, permeating and enveloping you. As you move around, that cocoon of confidence will move with you.

Step 7: Visualize the future unfolding from that cue moment. See yourself behaving with confidence and all the other qualities you've selected.

Step 8: When the cue moment arrives for real, visualize the circle on the floor, step into it and go and do what you have to do.

Insight

Remember that NLP makes the presupposition that people already have all the resources they need. You should try hard to find the necessary qualities within you. If you can't, visualize another person who embodies the necessary qualities – perhaps a character in a film.

Swishing confidence

In the last chapter you learned about Swishing – creating an emotion with one image and then quickly substituting a new image which, as a result, acquires the same emotional charge as the first. Here we're going to use it for confidence, which means you can use it as an alternative to the Circle of Confidence above, or as a supplement to it. The more techniques you have at your disposal and the more frequently you use them, the more powerful the effect.

For the following Swish exercise, find yourself somewhere comfortable and quiet. Propping yourself up on your bed is ideal. If you prefer, you can practise Steps 1, 3 and 4 on separate occasions. Once you're proficient at them you can put the whole procedure together and run through it in its entirety, from beginning to end, the necessary number of times.

Insight

This is a particularly difficult visualization, but hopefully you've been practising your visualization technique ever since Chapter 1. If not, turn back to that chapter and study the basics of the method. Some people have a very highly developed ability to 'see' images created in their own brains. Other people find it very hard. If you're having problems, I've found that thinking of photographs can be a better way to begin than by trying to recall the people or events themselves. And when it comes to visualizing *yourself*, photographs and home movies are better than trying to remember what you saw in the mirror.

HAVE A GO

Step 1: Your first task is to think of the kind of situation in which you need to have more confidence. A situation in which you have felt inadequate in the past and which you know is going to occur again in the future. When it does, you don't want to feel inadequate any more. You want to feel that you will acquit yourself well in your own eyes and in the eyes of other people. Really enter into that unsatisfactory experience. See, hear, smell, taste and touch as much of it as possible. If anybody is saying anything, or you're saying anything, whether out loud or in your head, take note of it. Also note where in your body you experience those feelings of inadequacy. Perhaps in your stomach? Take your time over this. This is the cue image.

Step 2: Clear the screen. This is a little bit like eating a small piece of bread before going on to taste the next wine. The idea is simply to wipe the images from Step 1 so that your mind is ready for the next visualization. If you find it difficult to clear your head, try reciting your telephone number backwards.

Step 3: Now you're going to build an image of yourself the way you'd *like* to be. The way you'd look and feel if you had complete mastery of the cue image situation and *had already successfully dealt with it*. This is the 'you' that, in fact, you're going to become very shortly. We'll call this version 'wonderful you'. Spend plenty of time building the image of 'wonderful you'. What is 'wonderful you' wearing? How is 'wonderful you' standing or moving? What sort of look does 'wonderful you' have on his or her face? Carry on until you feel admiration for 'wonderful you'. Again, take your time. There's no rush. Finally, give 'wonderful you' something to say that really encapsulates how you'd like to feel after having triumphed. It could be, 'I'm the master of this situation' or 'I never fail' or 'Easy!' or whatever you want.

Step 4: Take the image of 'wonderful you' and compress it into a sparkling dot. Place the dot into a blank screen and then let it grow and grow until it fills the screen. Hear 'wonderful you' speaking the words you decided in Step 3. Repeat this step over and over until you can reliably conjure up the sparkling dot and expand it. This is the hardest step in the visualization for most people and you may have to practise it for a while.

Step 5: Place the sparkling dot into the centre of the cue image from Step 1 and Swish. Make that bothersome cue image fade and disintegrate while the sparkling dot gets bigger and brighter and clearer. If you already know what success would look like, then visualize 'wonderful you' behaving in that way in the expanded dot. For example, if you were nervous about a snowboarding manoeuvre, you could visualize 'wonderful you' perfectly emulating what you've seen experts do. On the other hand, if you don't know the solution then just visualize 'wonderful you' speaking the words from Step 3.

Step 6: Create a break by having a completely blank screen appear.

Step 7: Repeat Steps 4 to 6, getting faster and faster. It's impossible to say how many times will be necessary. Some people find two or three times are enough, others need ten and still others twenty.

Step 8: Try to recall the original cue image. If you can't, or if you can only do so with a struggle, then the process has worked. Never again let that negative cue image cloud your belief in yourself. Now go and test your new attitude in the real world.

Insight

You may well have difficulty manipulating that 'sparkling dot'. If so, just try swapping over (Swishing) the image you want in place of the image you don't want – that is, the cue image you created in Step 1. You may find it easier to create that mental picture of the 'wonderful you' if you can find a suitable reference on a DVD and play it over and over again.

The New Behaviour Generator

So now you're up, you're motivated and you're confident. But how would you like that confidence to manifest itself? How precisely do you want to behave? What do you actually want to *do*?

You can use the New Behaviour Generator to translate that feeling of confidence into a whole scenario. It can be short and simple, or you can make it as long and detailed as you like. You can test alternative moves, rehearse the one you like until it's perfect and then install it as a permanent behaviour.

HAVE A GO

Step 1: Identify the new behaviour you would like to have. For this example, let's say you want to be more expansive and charismatic.

Step 2: You are the director of a movie in which you are also the star. As the director, give instructions to yourself about the way you should behave. Watch yourself exhibit the new behaviour. In your role as director, make any corrections or changes you think necessary.

Step 3: Once you're satisfied, step into the movie and experience what it's like to have this new way of behaving, as seen through your own eyes as the star. Not only see but, of course, hear everything and feel what it's like. (In other words, you've now switched from third position to first position, from dissociation to association – if you've forgotten about multiple perspectives, refer to Chapter 2.) Note the reaction of other people. Is it what you want it to be? Also check that this new behaviour really is suitable for you.

Step 4: If you're not happy with anything, return to your role as director, make the necessary changes and repeat Step 3.

Step 5: Use future pacing. Visualize a situation in the future where you will want to behave in this new way. Look for a cue that could be used to trigger the behaviour automatically. For example, it might be the door to your boss's office, your partner shouting or your children squabbling. Imagine yourself seeing or hearing the cue and immediately adopting the new behaviour. Play this 'film' as often as necessary until the new behaviour feels natural.

Step 6: Use the new behaviour in a real situation.

MAKING A REAL FILM

Not everybody can visualize well enough to make the New Behaviour Generator work as well as they'd like. If you find you're having problems, you could take on the roles of director and actor for real.

HAVE A GO

Step 1: Get hold of a DVD version of a film in which you've seen the type of behaviour you'd like to copy. Find a segment in which your character exhibits the behaviour and watch it several times.

Step 2: Get hold of a video camera of some sort. If you're completely uninhibited you can ask someone to film you. Otherwise, set it up on a tripod – it will be a great help if you can connect it to your TV which will then become a monitor. If you can't set up a monitor then you'll have to get by as best you can. (Without a monitor, you may find that on your first attempt you've cut half of your head off or something like that. Never mind – just make the necessary adjustments and try again.)

Step 3: Rehearse the behaviour then set the camera rolling.

Step 4: Watch the 'rushes'.

Step 5: Keep filming and watching and filming and watching until you think you've got the result you want. If necessary, inspire yourself by watching the original film again.

Step 6: Try out the new behaviour for real.

How to anchor a behaviour

Suppose you'd like to respond to certain situations in a particular way but just can't rely upon yourself to do that. It might be that you'd like to feel confident when making presentations, or patient when teaching your children, or resolute in the face of opposition. The problem is that, in the real world, it's so easy to become nervous when you have to perform in front of other people, so easy to become irritable with children, so easy to cave in when confronted by a forceful personality.

Wouldn't it be useful if you could actually program yourself so the desired response was *automatic*? So that no matter what self-doubts or negative emotions you had, you nevertheless could accomplish the task, and perform it to a high standard. Well you can certainly help yourself by using the technique of 'anchoring'.

Jargon buster – anchoring

In their book *Trance-formations*, Bandler and Grinder say that '**anchoring** refers to the tendency for any one element of an experience to bring back the entire experience'. NLP uses that perfectly natural phenomenon to create artificial triggers.

Insight

An anchor is a development of the conditioned stimulus described by Ivan Pavlov (1849–1936) in his famous work on the training of dogs. He used a metronome to call dogs to their food and, very soon, the dogs began salivating in response to the metronome. Most people are not very astonished to learn of Pavlov's findings. It's what would be expected. Nevertheless, his research has significant implications for learning and especially for the creation of automatic behaviours. Anchoring is NLP's version of the conditioned stimulus.

All kinds of things can be anchors. For example, a certain piece of music might always make you feel romantic because it was playing when you first met the person you're in love with. The smell of coffee might make you feel warm and gregarious because you associate it with the friendly bustle of a certain café. And the mere sight of a comedian making a trademark gesture might make you laugh, not because the gesture itself is funny but because it's an anchor that recalls all the previous times the comedian made you laugh. This is what rituals are all about. They're anchors that come to evoke particular *emotions*.

There are also all kinds of stimuli to which we've learned to carry out certain *actions* automatically. If you've ever rehearsed a play you've probably used anchors. Someone gives you a 'cue' and you then automatically disgorge the lines you learned. If you're driving a car and you see brake lights go on ahead of you, without even thinking, you take your foot off the accelerator and move it to the brake pedal. In this example, brake lights are the trigger (or anchor) and the action of braking is the programmed response. (Notice, however, that the anchor doesn't actually *compel* you to brake – you retain your freedom to perform a different action if you judge that the situation demands it.)

Insight

Think back to the things you do before facing various sorts of demanding situations. Are there, perhaps, little rituals you perform that, in reality, have no practical benefit but make you feel 'right'? These are 'anchors'. Make a list of them. Later, using the technique below, you can learn to amplify them.

Choosing anchors

Skilled hypnotists can use quite unrelated stimuli as anchors, but when you're using this technique on yourself it will work better if the anchor is as natural and logical as possible.

Ideally, an anchor should meet the following conditions:

▶ *It has genuine meaning or an intrinsic connection with the desired emotion, belief or action (in the case of the 'brake light*

anchor' we know it only comes on when the driver in front
presses his brake pedal and slows down).

▶ *You want to respond to the anchor (otherwise you'll collide*
  with the car in front).
▶ *It should be easy to activate, but not to activate accidentally*
  (everyone can press a brake pedal).
▶ *You're fully capable of responding to the anchor (again,*
  everyone can press a brake pedal).
▶ *It should combine two or preferably three senses (the brake*
  light anchor fails on this – the addition of an audible signal
  would be an improvement).

HAVE A GO

In the example that follows, we'll be anchoring a feeling of
patience. But you can adapt this procedure for anything you want.

Step 1: Choose your anchors. For patience, I'm going to suggest
you stroke your chin, which involves the optimum three senses.
It is:

▶ *a visual anchor – the sight of your hand coming up to your*
  chin and moving in front of your chin
▶ *an audible anchor – the sound of your fingers against the skin*
  of your face; behind the concealment of your hand you could
  also whisper the word 'patience'
▶ *a kinaesthetic anchor – the feeling of your fingers against the*
  skin of your face.

Step 2: Think of a time when you felt truly serene, calm,
imperturbable and – above all – patient. Remember the NLP
presupposition that we already have within us all the resources
we need. However, if you really can't recall such a time, then
imagine the feeling or recall a film in which someone you admire
exhibited supreme patience.

Step 3: Revel in that feeling of patience. See, hear, touch, taste and
smell everything to do with that patience. Spin it up as described
in Chapter 1.

Step 4: Just *before* your feeling of patience reaches its peak, set your anchors by gently stroking your chin and whispering the word 'patience'. Repeat the process several times.

Step 5: Future pace by visualizing a scene that demands patience and watch yourself responding with patience.

Step 6: As soon as possible, deliberately seek out a situation that will test your patience a little. Fire your anchors. Over the next few days, keep on experiencing irritating situations and keep on firing your anchors. You will need to deal successfully with maybe a score of situations before the anchor will become permanent and automatic.

Insight

The setting of anchors can be quite an art.

As I emphasized in Step 4, you need to do it just *before* the emotion you're dealing with reaches peak intensity. In that way, the anchor will be associated with strong and growing emotion. If you set your anchor *after* peak emotion then it will be associated with a decline in feeling, which is not the result you want at all.

The anchor also needs to be pure. In other words, if you're, say, feeling sceptical when you try this procedure then you'll be anchoring patience contaminated with scepticism – again, not the result you want.

Increasing the power of anchors

The more you use an anchor, the more powerful it becomes. We're all familiar with the way sportsmen punch the air or do a little dance when they've scored. What they're doing is 'stacking' an anchor. Each time they perform that ritual they add the power of that new victory to all their previous victories. That, in turn, creates the psychological impression of an unstoppable momentum of success.

You can use this technique for all kinds of things. The key to it is that you must really energize your anchor. You need to experience that feeling of triumph (or whatever you have chosen) to the maximum and focus it into your ritual, just as a magnifying glass focuses the sun's rays in one spot. When you need to 'psych yourself up', you perform your ritual and flood yourself with the feelings you've anchored.

Rewriting your future

So far we've dealt with fairly short-term issues: how you'd like to feel when you wake up; motivating yourself to get going on something right now; generating the confidence to try. But you also need a strategy for the future. How do you see yourself in a year's time, for example? In five years? In ten years? And how will you get there?

You should be beginning to realize that NLP has the tools to help you build the future you want. Let's try to set a course for one of your goals right now. Of course, it has to be something that actually is achievable. It has to be something over which *you* have control (because you can influence other people but you can't control *them*). And it must be something that won't have a detrimental effect on you or other people – carry out an ecology check as described in Chapter 1.

I want you to say your goal right now out loud, but it must be expressed in a particular way. Remember, as we saw in the previous chapter:

> *Goals must always be phrased in positive terms.*

If you've ever listened to the Oscars ceremony, you've probably heard actors saying how they've dreamed of winning and how they've rehearsed their acceptance speech many times over the years. This next technique employs a similar process, but taken to a higher level.

HAVE A GO

This method is rather like the 'reverse engineering' of a machine – something that's often done by companies that want to beat the competition. They buy a product from another company and take it apart to see how it was made. Similarly, if you want to work out how to make a goal come true, it's better to work backwards from the goal than forwards from where you are now.

Step 1: Picture the scene of your future success in as much detail as possible, noticing the colours, the sounds, the smells and so on.

Step 2: Put yourself into that scene and see yourself achieving your goal. Watch and listen as if you were at the cinema.

Step 3: In your role as director, improve the impact of the 'film' in every way you can. Perhaps you can use more close-ups. Different camera angles. Slow motion. Freeze-frames. Music for emphasis. A voice-over saying what a great thing you've achieved. Really revel in the whole thing. See it. Hear it. Touch it. Taste it. Smell it. It's real.

Step 4: Look backwards from the scene of your triumph to where you are today. See the road that brought you to your goal.

Step 5: Slowly amble back along the side of the road and identify the various steps that brought you to your goal. Don't rush. There could have been all kinds of factors and you need to identify every one. Ask yourself what personal qualities you brought to bear to reach your goal. What actions did you take? What other people were involved? How did you relate to them? As you go, write down all the steps in sequence.

Step 6: Once back in the present, consult your list and begin putting it into action.

Insight

I find it very important to get a diary and mark target dates in it. Otherwise it's all too easy to let things slip. For example, let's say that in your visualization you've achieved your goal by Christmas and today is March 1st. And let's say that as you stroll back along the road in the visualization you identify ten separate stages. Then mark in your diary that each stage must be completed by the end of the month and that the whole process must be completed by December 25th. Better still, use a wall chart so you can see the process at a glance.

SELF-HYPNOSIS FOR CONFIDENCE

The Betty Erickson self-hypnosis method can also be used to help you look at things more positively. If you've forgotten how to put yourself into a trance, refer back to Chapter 1. When you're stating the purpose of your self-hypnosis (Step 3) say something like: 'I am entering into a trance for the purpose of allowing my unconscious mind to make the adjustments that will help me feel more confident (or whatever it is you wish to feel).' When you come to the visualization (Steps 5f and 5g), imagine a scene in which you are behaving in the way you want.

10 THINGS TO REMEMBER

1   It's what you program into yourself as you fall asleep that determines how you'll feel when you wake up.

2   For any given situation, it helps to know if you're the sort of person who is predominantly motivated away from things or whether you're motivated towards.

3   You can 'borrow' motivation by Swishing it from something else.

4   Infants have no fear of failure, so be 'infantile'.

5   The Circle of Confidence and the Swish technique can both be used to increase your confidence.

6   The New Behaviour Generator is a way of installing new behaviour by becoming the star and director of an imaginary film.

7   It's possible to anchor a desired behaviour so that it can be triggered automatically.

8   The more you use an anchor, the more powerful it becomes.

9   You can 'reverse engineer' any goal you want to work out how it can be achieved.

10 You can use the Betty Erickson self-hypnosis method to increase your confidence.

HOW AM I GETTING ON?

▶ *Have you tried programming yourself just before you go to sleep?*

▶ *If so, did you succeed?*

▶ *Have you worked out whether your motivation is predominantly* away *or* towards?

▶ *Have you succeeded in Swishing motivation from something you love to do to something you hate doing?*

▶ *Have you succeeded in increasing your confidence by either the Circle of Confidence or the Swish technique, or both?*

▶ *Have you starred in and directed your own 'film' and installed a new behaviour as a result?*

▶ *Have you succeeded in creating an anchor?*

▶ *Have you successfully used that anchor to trigger an automatic behaviour?*

▶ *Have you reverse engineered an ambition?*

▶ *Have you used the Betty Erickson method to make yourself feel more confident?*

If you answered 'No' to four or more questions, then read through the relevant parts of the chapter once more and try the techniques again. The more you practise these visualizations, the better you'll get at them – and the more powerful the effects will be.

6

Transform your health

In this chapter you will learn:
- *how you can help cure yourself*
- *how you can give up bad habits and acquire healthy ones*
- *how you can avoid harmful stress and learn to relax*
- *how to help control pain.*

The mind and body are parts of the same system.

NLP presupposition

Back in the early days, Bandler and Grinder studied the data on placebos and concluded they were provenly effective 20 per cent of the time. Apparently, the two men joked about selling bottles of 'Placebo' which would escape the normal regulatory approval for medicines because the pills would be inert. Later they would release 'Placebo Plus – now with even more inert ingredients'.

NLP is hardly alone in taking the view that the mind and the body form one system. Let's call it the 'bodymind'. Our bodies affect the way we think, and the way we think affects our bodies. Since NLP is all about the way we think, especially at the unconscious level, so it should also be very good at improving our health in all kinds of ways.

The placebo effect has been known for thousands of years. It doesn't mean, of course, that an illness is 'all in the mind'. It means the *cure* for the illness is in the mind. And that's perfectly logical. After all, the blueprint for our bodies, our DNA, is contained in every cell. Theoretically, we should be capable of not only repairing any damage but of actually recreating any parts of our bodies that we need to, working from that blueprint.

In reality, our bodyminds don't do a bad job. We can't re-grow limbs, but doctors estimate that about 80 per cent of medical problems do get better entirely on their own – or would do so if we'd let them.

So why isn't it 100 per cent of the time? The placebo effect suggests that the bodymind can usefully be given a bit of a pep talk. That it can be cajoled into trying harder: 'Look, 80 per cent is okay but if you really made an effort you could hit 90 per cent.'

But can the mind really increase the body's existing natural ability to recover?

The placebo effect

It was in 1955 in *The Powerful Placebo* that H. K. Beecher analysed 15 clinical trials and concluded that 35 per cent of patients were relieved by the placebo effect alone. While pharmaceutical companies scrambled to defend themselves, some subsequent researchers were even more enthusiastic, putting the effect as high as 50 or even 60 per cent for certain conditions. The placebo effect became a commonplace, widely accepted by everyone.

Until, that is, certain meticulous researchers began revisiting the original studies. And they were struck by a huge hole in the data. When certain medical interventions were compared with placebos, they were found to be no more effective. But, in many cases, no one had thought to compare the placebo effect itself with anything else. In May 2001, in *The New England Journal Of Medicine*, the Danish researchers Asbjorn Hrobjartsson and Peter C Gotzsche concluded that a great deal of placebo research was flawed because the scientists had compared the placebos with genuine treatments *but not with no treatment at all*. In other words, certain drugs and surgical interventions may have proved no better than placebos, but there was no proof that the placebos were better than doing nothing.

So where do we stand now?

The consensus view seems to be that although the placebo effect may not be as widespread and powerful as many had thought, it is nevertheless a genuine phenomenon. Every doctor and nurse has tales of patients who recovered against the odds because of their positive mental attitudes. And the evidence is more than anecdotal. Among the scientific studies widely accepted is one in which doctors successfully eliminated warts by painting them with an inert dye and telling their patients that the warts would be gone by the time the dye wore off. In another reliable study, researchers found that asthmatics could dilate their airways if they believed the placebo they were being given was a bronchodilator. And numerous experiments have proven that placebos can reduce the perception of pain.

The placebo effect, then, is real – even if it's not as significant as had been supposed. It's caused by anything that, despite being inert, somehow increases the power of the body's natural defences. It could be a sugar pill, it could be an impressive piece of otherwise worthless machinery, it could be mysterious spells… and it could be NLP.

Recovering with NLP

Richard Bandler recounts how, when he had a stroke, a doctor in the emergency ward told him: 'No matter what anyone says to you, no matter who they are, I am telling you, you can make a full recovery.'

A few days later another doctor told Bandler he would be paralysed for the rest of his life. But Bandler chose, instead, to think of what he had been told in the emergency ward: 'I would focus every fibre in my soul,' he wrote, 'in being able to first move my toes and then my feet and then my knees...'.

He didn't think about what he *couldn't* do. That would have created a sense of failure. Instead, he focused on what he was succeeding at. Moving just one toe was a success and became the platform for moving two toes. And so on.

HAVE A GO

Step 1: Deal with any negative prognostications by giving the speakers voices you don't trust. (If you don't remember how to do that, turn back to Chapter 4 – it's the same procedure as for dealing with a negative inner voice.) Once you've got rid of that negativity, never think about those prognostications again.

Step 2: Promise yourself you *will* make a full recovery. Think of all the difficult situations you've come through in the past. Take this determination and spin it up (as described in Chapter 1).

Step 3: Visualize yourself getting better and better.

Step 4: Visualize a time in the future when you *are* fully recovered. Revel in that experience. See, feel, hear, taste and smell what it's like to be fully recovered. Adjust the submodalities to make the experience of being fully recovered as vivid as possible.

Step 5: Repeat Steps 2–4 several times a day until you *are* better.

Insight

Every journey, as they say, starts with a small step, and one of the keys to this is to focus on those small improvements. You don't let yourself get awed by the immensity of the task ahead. Simply focus on what you have to do right now and you do it as well as you can. Then focus on the next step. And so on. Don't make comparisons with the things other people can do. Only make comparisons with yourself yesterday and last week and last month to celebrate

(Contd)

the progress you're making (known in NLP as self-to-self comparisons). But always have the visualization of that ultimate goal (Step 4) so your unconscious knows what you're aiming at.

When you have more minor ailments, a simple visualization when you're going off to sleep at night can help. Bedtime is a good moment for this because it gives you good access to your unconscious just when your bodymind is best able to repair itself. For example, let's say that you've damaged your Achilles tendon.

HAVE A GO
Step 1: Get yourself nicely relaxed in bed and begin drifting off to sleep.

Step 2: Focus on an image of health and identify the submodalities. Is the sun shining, for example? Is your skin shining? Is there a particular feeling in your body? Do you hear anything?

Step 3: Set a target for the bodymind to aim at, by visualizing yourself as completely healthy. Turn up all the submodalities associated with health. See that the part or parts of your body associated with your current problem (in this case your Achilles tendon) are entirely sound and well.

Step 4: Visualize yourself saying something along the following lines: 'I am well. My Achilles tendon (or whatever part of the body is affected) is completely healthy.' You can go on to describe how wonderful it is, how strong, elastic and controlled (or whatever).

Step 5: Continue like this until you fall asleep.

Motivating yourself for healthy living

Some people find it very enjoyable to lead a healthy life. Others find it rather difficult.

If you need motivation to live more healthily, one NLP solution is to Swish. The idea is to make yourself feel good about healthy living and at the same time feel bad about not being healthy.

HAVE A GO
The following example explains how you can motivate yourself to take regular exercise, but you could equally adapt the technique for many other aspects of healthy living.

Step 1: Think of how you will be if you don't exercise. Imagine yourself getting fatter, stiffer, more out of breath, less energetic and prematurely aged. Spend time over this. Turn up the submodalities so you really experience all those problems.

Step 2: Think of something you enjoy doing *regularly*. It could be anything but for promoting exercise, it will work better if it's also something physical – like taking a shower. Really revel in the enjoyable physical sensations of the warm water trickling all over your body. Try to identify the submodalities associated with the regularity of that pleasure. Why is it something you do automatically? Once you have those submodalities, turn them up to the maximum.

Step 3: Generate an image of you doing your chosen exercise and immediately Swish it into the position occupied by the image you created in Step 2. The submodalities associated with taking a regular shower should attach themselves to the idea of regular exercise. Revel in this exercise image and thoroughly enjoy the physical pleasure of it.

Step 4: Repeat the Swish several times until you feel really positive about exercise as a normal part of your daily routine.

Step 5: Future pace. Visualize yourself some time in the future, just completing your regular exercise, feeling wonderful and looking healthier, slimmer, younger and more charismatic.

Step 6: Begin your exercise programme. Repeat the motivation exercise as necessary.

Giving up isn't so hard to do

Being healthy means doing certain things. It also means not doing
other things, such as smoking, overeating or drinking large quantities
of alcohol.

Here's how you can motivate yourself *not* to do something.

HAVE A GO

Step 1: Think of five occasions on which your habit or addiction
made you frightened for your health or disgusted with your
behaviour. If alcohol is the problem, for example, then you might
recall wasting large sums of money, saying hurtful things you later
regretted, vomiting, having a terrible hangover, and being unable
to do your job properly. If the problem is smoking, you could
visualize the smoke funnelling into your lungs and leaving behind
a fine layer of carcinogenic dust, having teeth removed because
smoking has caused gum disease, being rebuffed by someone you
were attracted to because they found your breath too disgusting,
and so on. Experience those images to the full. Really see, feel,
hear, taste and smell everything.

Step 2: Make a movie of your habit or addiction by running the
five scenes in your mind, one after the other.

Step 3: Keep running them faster and faster until you really feel
you want to end this behaviour for ever.

———————————————— **xxx** ————————————————

Having developed motivation, your next step is to believe that you
can succeed in giving up. The old joke is that giving up is easy: 'I've

done it dozens of times.' The problem in real life is that if you've tried several times and failed then you may have lost confidence that you can succeed. The next two visualizations are aimed at increasing your belief.

HAVE A GO
Step 1: Think of something in which you take pride that you already are a 'non' – for example, a non-drug-user or non-violent or something like that. Think how good it is to be a 'non' in that case. Really revel in and enjoy the self-respect you have for yourself as a 'non'.

Step 2: Now visualize yourself as a non-smoker (or non-whatever) and immediately attach to that image the same feelings of pride and self-respect you generated in Step 1.

Step 3: Repeat until you really do begin to think of yourself as a non-smoker (or non-whatever).

―――――――――――――――――**xxx**―――――――――――――――――

HAVE A GO
Step 1: Think of an occasion when you had a really powerful desire to give in to a temptation but nevertheless overcame it. This is Image 1.

Step 2: Now visualize a scene in which you are being offered a cigarette (or whatever it is) and quickly Swish it into the submodalities of Image 1. Now see yourself refusing what you were being offered, just as you overcame temptation in Image 1.

Step 3: Repeat until you feel a conviction that you could resist your habit or addiction.

―――――――――――――――――――――――――

Redirecting a craving

A craving can be a very powerful thing and sometimes it can be better not to fight it head on. Instead, like a judoka, you can turn the energy of the craving against itself. Or rather, switch it to something else that's positive for you, rather than negative.

Step 1: Think of something the acts as a trigger to your craving.

Step 2: Begin to run a mental movie from that trigger point and then almost immediately white it out, just like a television or cinema screen going blank.

Step 3: Replace the image with another in which you are free of the craving and very happy to be free of it.

> **Insight**
>
> The idea of this procedure is that your craving should be detached from its normal object (cigarettes, alcohol or whatever) and be reattached to the state of freedom. In other words, you no longer crave what you were addicted to but, instead, crave freedom from it. As an option you could visualize an alternative, desirable behaviour and reattach your craving to that. For example, it could be that you now crave running or swimming.

Modelling for health

If you find it hard to believe that life can be worth living without large quantities of alcohol, or chocolate, or fat, or if you find it hard to believe that exercise can be fun, then it might be worthwhile modelling someone who has a healthy lifestyle. If you grew up in an unhealthy household then being unhealthy may seem normal to you. You need to replace that concept with a new model.

Do you know anybody who has an especially healthy lifestyle? It needs to be someone you admire, otherwise you'll only confirm your own prejudices against healthy living (for example, that healthy people are boring).

As usual with modelling, just try to absorb their way of being without asking too many questions initially. Here are some of the things you might pay attention to:

- ▶ *how many hours they sleep*
- ▶ *how much exercise they take*
- ▶ *how many portions of fruit and vegetables they eat*
- ▶ *how much alcohol they drink*
- ▶ *how often they get stressed and angry.*

In this instance, the point of modelling is not for you to pioneer new ways of achieving optimum health (thousands of researchers are already engaged in that) but for you to be able to experience the fact that there are people who can be healthy *and happy*.

Staying healthy

Some people seem to get ill much more often than others. Whatever is going around they're always the ones to get it and they have far more days off work than anybody else. Why? Of course, there could be all kinds of reasons. But having a positive mental attitude certainly is a factor. This adaptation of the Circle of Confidence can help you remain fit when others around you are falling ill. I call it the Circle of Health.

Step 1: Search your memory for a time in the past when you felt especially healthy. Relive that feeling of health. Particularly notice the glow on your skin, the brightness of your eyes, and the energy that was oozing out of you.

Step 2: Imagine a circle on the floor. Take the health you experienced in Step 1 and pour it into the circle. Immediately the circle takes on a colour – the colour that, to you, is the colour of health. It also makes a noise. Maybe it's a humming sound or even music – again, it's whatever expresses health to you.

Step 3: Are there any other qualities you think will contribute to health? Maybe optimism? Maybe serenity? If so, repeat the procedure, also pouring those qualities into your circle.

Step 4: Step into the circle and visualize all those qualities rising up from the floor, permeating and enveloping you. As you move around so that cocoon of health will move with you, protecting you from whatever might threaten your wellbeing.

Step 5: Future pace. Imagine a time in the future when you're still within your Circle of Health. Make it at age 80 or 90 or even 100. See yourself still radiating health, your skin still glowing, your eyes still bright, your movements still agile and lively.

Dealing with stress

Stress can be both good and bad for your health. Let's say two of you face the same challenging situation. One of you is exhilarated; that's eustress or 'good stress'. The other is anxious and frightened; that's distress or 'bad stress'. One situation, two reactions. And in the long term two different health outcomes. While eustress is good for your health, distress is very, very bad.

When you suffer distress, among other things:

▶ *adrenaline and noradrenaline are released from the adrenal glands*
▶ *cortisol and other stress hormones are released into the blood*
▶ *blood pressure rises*
▶ *heart rate increases*
▶ *sugar and fat pour into the bloodstream.*

This is all preparation for what's known as the 'fight or flight' response. In modern life we normally do neither of those things and therefore we don't burn the sugar and the fat. The result over time is a long list of disorders from heartburn, headaches and allergies up to diabetes, heart disease and cancer.

There are various ways of ensuring you feel eustress rather than distress. For example, for a physical challenge the person who trains the hardest will cope the easiest. But there's always a mental aspect too. And that's where NLP comes in.

ANCHORING FOR RELAXATION

In Chapter 5 you learned how to Swish for confidence. When you feel confident, you automatically feel less stress – so that's a useful tool. In Chapter 5 you also learned about anchoring. If you've forgotten how to do it, turn back and re-read that section because we're now going to add to your repertoire with a way of anchoring relaxation. (You may also find that it relieves headaches.) Bear in mind that being relaxed is not the same thing as being inactive. You can still take steps to deal with the situation, but you'll do it without feeling distressed.

HAVE A GO

Step 1: Recall a time when you felt *incredibly* relaxed. Fully experience that sense of relaxation. Feel, see, hear, smell and taste the elements that made you that way. Identify the submodalities for relaxation.

Step 2: Create a break state by saying your telephone number backwards.

Step 3: Select three different kinds of anchors. A convenient kinaesthetic anchor might be stroking the sides of your face between your thumb and forefinger. An auditory anchor could simply be whispering the word 'relax' to yourself or recalling a tranquil piece of music (or both together). A visual anchor might be recalling the scene from Step 1.

Step 4: Re-experience the relaxation you created in Step 1. Take the submodalities for relaxation and adjust them until you're approaching the optimum level but not quite there. At that very moment, fire your three anchors.

Step 5: Create a break state by saying your telephone number backwards.

Step 6: Repeat Step 4 several times. On each occasion, try to improve the whole thing so that you feel more and more relaxed and your anchor-setting technique gets better and better.

Step 7: Fire your anchors. If you feel relaxed as a result then the procedure has worked.

Step 8: Future pace. Think of future potentially distressing situations in which you would like to feel more at ease. As you do so, fire your anchors. This will set things up for you so that when those situations come about you'll already be primed to become relaxed.

Step 9: Live life and whenever you encounter stressful situations for real, fire your anchors. The more often you repeat the procedure and the more often you use the anchors the more powerful the effect will be.

Insight

It can be difficult to *decrease* tension when you're thinking of *increasing* submodalities. The two ideas work against one another. That's why, in Step 4, I said 'adjust' the submodalities rather than 'increase' and why I've talked of the 'optimum' level rather than the 'maximum'.

SELF-HYPNOSIS FOR RELIEVING STRESS

You're now familiar with the Betty Erickson self-hypnosis technique. If you need to remind yourself of the details turn back to Chapter 1. When you're stating the purpose of your self-hypnosis (Step 3) say something like: 'I am entering into a trance for the purpose of allowing my unconscious mind to provide me with a period of time when I will feel utterly relaxed.' When you come to the visualization (Steps 5f and 5g), imagine the most happy, beautiful and restful scene that you can conjure up. For example, it might be floating in a lake of warm, blue water on a calm summer's day.

Pain control

There are various NLP techniques that can help control pain, either on their own or in conjunction with drugs.

REFRAMING FOR PAIN CONTROL

One way of dealing with pain is to reframe it using laughter. This would be known in NLP as a 'meaning' or 'content' reframe. The way it works is to do something to increase the pain a little and then laugh. It sounds ridiculous but it can help. Keep doing it until the pain doesn't seem so bad. The laughter doesn't necessarily make the pain go away but it can change the way you feel about it. (Indeed, there are even people who grow to *like* pain – we call them masochists.) Milton Erickson, whose hypnotic techniques we'll be examining in detail in the next few chapters, once helped an amputee suffering phantom limb pain simply by planting the suggestion that a phantom limb could equally be a source of pleasure.

OVERLOADING AND DISTRACTION

It's fairly well established that the conscious mind can only handle seven items (plus or minus two) at any time. Overloading the brain therefore means something has to be ignored and, with a bit of luck, it will be the pain.

Distraction works in a similar way but uses one very powerful stimulus instead of several lesser ones.

In fact, we're probably all familiar with this kind of phenomenon, receiving an injury but being completely unaware of it at the time because we're preoccupied by a task or by, say, the need to escape a fire or a crash or something like that.

Milton Erickson was once brought a woman dying of cancer. She told him she was sceptical of hypnosis but was willing to try anything because of the pain. 'Madam, I think I can convince you,' said Erickson. 'And you know how much pain you are suffering, how uncontrollable it is. If you saw a hungry tiger walking through that doorway, licking its chops and looking at you, how much pain would you feel?' The woman was so astonished at the question – so *distracted* – that she said, 'Not a bit – in fact, I'm not feeling any pain now, either.'

In another case, Erickson was brought a woman who suffered from severe, chronic hip pain. Erickson spoke to her at length about the different kinds of nerves that there are and how they work and as she began to get bored with the overload of information so he began to seed various ideas such as the way hands become calloused and insensitive with a lot of manual work. The woman then took that idea and made it her own, envisaging her nerve eventually becoming calloused through overuse. That concept helped her to reduce the sensation of pain.

HAVE A GO

If you're in pain and normal analgesics aren't providing complete relief, find yourself a task that is absolutely riveting and that requires various kinds of mental activity. What you choose will obviously depend very much on your personality. A game such as poker can be good because it involves all sorts of things such as remembering cards, reading the body language of the other players, taking conscious control of your own body language, and calculating how much to bet. Or you might like to try composing a tune and writing it down in some sort of notation. Or describing in detail *everything* you saw, heard, felt, tasted and smelt while looking at, say, a beautiful landscape on holiday last year.

SELF-HYPNOSIS FOR PAIN CONTROL

The Betty Erickson self-hypnosis technique can also be used to program yourself so that you feel less pain or are even pain-free for extended periods. The procedure is the same as described above (see Self-hypnosis for relieving stress) but you would say something like: 'I am entering into a trance for the purpose of allowing my unconscious mind to correct an error in my nervous system. Pain is a signal that something is wrong. I have received that message and everything that could be done is being done so there's no point now in continuing the pain.' When you come to the visualization (Steps 5f and 5g), imagine a scene in which you are serene and free of pain: for example, you might be floating in a warm bath.

An alternative approach would be to try to separate your mind from the pain your body is experiencing by saying something like this: 'I am entering into a trance so that I can hand over to my unconscious mind the task of separating, for a short while, the real me from my body. I will leave my body here in bed and the real me will go and watch television.'

10 THINGS TO REMEMBER

1   *The extent of the placebo effect remains controversial but there's no doubt that it exists.*

2   *NLP has various techniques for harnessing the placebo effect.*

3   *Focus on one step at a time but always promise yourself that you will make a full recovery.*

4   *If you find healthy living boring, the Swish technique can be used to increase your motivation.*

5   *Creating an internal movie of the negative effects of addiction can help you give up.*

6   *Visualization can be used to increase your belief in your ability to give up things that damage your health and to redirect cravings in new, positive directions.*

7   *Modelling can give you a whole new outlook on healthy living.*

8   *The Circle of Health can help you develop a positive mindset.*

9   *Bad stress (or distress) is extremely dangerous for your health: anchoring can help you relax.*

10 *You can help control pain using the techniques of reframing, overload, distraction and self-hypnosis.*

HOW AM I GETTING ON?

▶ *If you've been ill, have you been able to deal with negative voices?*

▶ *If you've been ill, have you been able to concentrate on one step at a time while retaining a belief in a full recovery?*

▶ *Have you used the Swish technique to install regular, healthy habits?*

▶ *Have you turned yourself off any bad habits by creating an internal movie of the damage they're doing?*

▶ *Do you really believe you can give up unhealthy habits?*

▶ *Have you successfully redirected a harmful craving to something more positive?*

▶ *Have you spent time with someone who leads a really healthy lifestyle?*

▶ *Have you used the Circle of Health to develop confidence in your bodymind?*

▶ *Have you successfully used anchoring to relax in what would otherwise have been a distressing situation?*

▶ *Have you succeeded in reducing your perception of pain or even of making it go away altogether?*

If you haven't yet experimented with at least five techniques then read through the relevant parts of the chapter once more and give them a go. Your health is a priority.

7

Transform your powers of persuasion

In this chapter you will learn:
- *how to build rapport*
- *how to influence the unconscious minds of others*
- *how to be persuasive.*

> *You cannot not communicate.*
>
> NLP presupposition

In 1975, Bandler, Grinder and Gregory Bateson all lived in apartments at 1000 Alba Road, Ben Lomand, California. Bateson (1904–80) was by then famous as a multi-talented anthropologist, social scientist and linguist. Following the circulation of *The Structure of Magic, Volume 1* in manuscript form, Bateson invited the two younger men over for a chat. Evidently impressed, he later suggested they turned their modelling skills on Dr Milton H Erickson, described by Grinder as a 'renegade physician psychiatrist'. Bandler and Grinder, already familiar with Erickson's books, were only too happy to agree.

Erickson not only used formal hypnosis to treat a range of problems but also 'casual hypnosis'. That's to say, he connected with people's unconscious minds using some of the techniques of hypnosis but without inducing what might be called a 'formal trance'. As a result of modelling Erickson (using the method described in Chapter 3), Bandler and Grinder went on to develop many of the techniques of NLP – including what they called the Milton Model (from Erickson's first name).

The Milton Model is a powerful technique for influencing people – not in the usual way by asking direct questions and giving direct orders – but by behaving almost in the opposite manner, telling stories, and saying things that are vague and ambiguous. In this chapter we'll be looking at Erickson's informal techniques as they can be used in everyday life. In the next chapter we'll be seeing how they, and other techniques, can be used in your most important relationship. And in Chapter 9 we'll take a look at formal hypnosis.

How ethical it is to use these techniques is something for you to decide, according to the circumstances. Of course Erickson used them to help people overcome problems, for which they had willingly come to consult him. In the cut and thrust of the business world you might also see them as legitimate. But at home, with people you love and who trust you, it would depend very much on your intentions. It has to be said that these techniques cannot force anyone to do anything. They just add to your persuasive powers.

Establishing rapport

The first thing any hypnotherapist has to do is to establish rapport. And the same generally applies whenever one person wants to influence another. Of course, it's *possible* to influence someone when there's no rapport but that influence tends to be negative. That's to say, if somebody doesn't like you or is in competition with you, they're apt to think or do the opposite to whatever you propose. In which case, *you'll* have to propose the opposite of what you really want. That gets complicated.

Far more straightforward is to get the other person on your side by establishing a friendly sense of trust. If you respond to other people in a way that's positive, uncritical, non-judgemental – and above all demonstrate that you're *like* them – then, inevitably, they will like you.

One of the ways in which NLP establishes rapport is through matching and mirroring (see Chapter 1). Just to remind you, matching means approximating another person's body language, while mirroring means doing *exactly* what the other person does, as if you are a mirror.

In fact, to a certain extent we all match and mirror unconsciously when we want to be liked by other people. NLP proposes that you do it *consciously*. In order to do it consciously, you first have to identify the key things the other person is doing. As we saw in Chapter 1, this is known in NLP as *calibrating*.

Calibration is something we all do all the time, to a certain extent. When we walk into a room and feel we could 'cut the atmosphere with a knife' we're calibrating. In fact, most of us aren't consciously aware of much of the body language involved in everyday life. We simply absorb it unconsciously and react accordingly. But if you're going to make practical use of people's body language, you need to get into the habit of analysing it. You also have to know how to use it yourself.

Hypnotherapists have to be very aware of the effect they're having. They have to know when someone is genuinely in a trance or merely pretending to be in trance. They have to know when someone's going deeper and when they're coming out. They have to know when someone is visualizing something. They have to know when the visualization is pleasurable and when it's painful. They have to know when the words they're saying are working and when they're creating resistance.

This ability to calibrate is known in NLP as 'sensory acuity'. Here are some fun exercises to develop your own sensory acuity. Obviously you're going to be looking out for facial expression but also more subtle signals, such as eye movements, posture, breathing and muscle tone.

HAVE A GO
Step 1: Ask a friend some simple questions that require only 'Yes' or 'No' answers.

Step 2: Note the body language that goes with 'Yes' and the body language that goes with 'No'.

Step 3: Now pose further questions, asking your friend not to reply out loud but simply to *think* 'Yes' or 'No'. From your observations of their body language you should be able to say accurately what the correct answers are.

———————————————— xxx ————————————————

This is one of the easiest calibrating exercises because most people will give, at least, a slight nod for a 'Yes' and a slight shake for a 'No'. Other signs might be tipping the head forward for a 'Yes' and back for a 'No', or warmer eyes for a 'Yes' and colder eyes for a 'No'.

HAVE A GO
Step 1: When you're next talking with someone, say something inoffensive about them you know is *not* true. Calibrate.

Step 2: Follow up with something inoffensive you know *is* true. Calibrate.

Step 3: Repeat this a few times until you've identified all the body language that goes with incorrect and correct statements.

For example, you might say: 'If I remember correctly your partner works for an oil company' or 'Didn't you once live in South America?'

———————————————— xxx ————————————————

HAVE A GO
Step 1: Ask a friend to think of someone he or she likes. Calibrate.

Step 2: Ask the friend to think of someone he or she hates. Calibrate.

Step 3: Repeat until you've identified all the body language.

Step 4: When you've got that clear, tell your friend that you're going to ask various questions about these two people but that you *don't* want your friend to tell you the answers. Instead, *you* will tell your friend the answers. All your friend has to do is look at you and nod when the answer is ready.

Step 5: Ask your friend questions, that require comparisons to be made between the person liked and the person hated. For example, you could ask: 'Which one has the largest feet?', 'Which one has the most freckles?' or 'Which one has the largest nose?' This works best if you ask questions that require your friend to conjure up images before answering. (A question such as 'Which one is tallest?' may be answered without much thought if the height difference is significant, and therefore without much change in body language.)

Step 6: After putting each question, observe your friend closely. He or she will think of one person then the other as the comparison is made. The answer will be the person your friend is thinking of just before looking at you and nodding – and you'll know which one that is by calibrating.

Insight

If you can't see any difference in your friend's body language, ask him or her to think of the person they love the most in the world and then the most revolting and unpleasant person. That should cause the body language to be a little more visible. You could also subtly encourage your friend to be more expressive by being very expressive yourself.

HAVE A GO

This crystal ball exercise is a lot of fun, but to really test your skills you'll need to try it out on people you don't know very well.

Step 1: Conversationally, make a few observations that require 'Yes/No' answers so you can observe your subject's body language.

Step 2: Cup your hands and say that you have a crystal ball there. Move it gently up and down in time with the subject's breathing.

Step 3: Now make an opening statement such as, 'I see someone very important to you.' Pause to let the subject think of someone, then say either 'It's a man' or 'It's a woman'. If the subject's body language shows agreement, move on to the next statement. If the subject's body language shows disagreement, cover yourself by saying, 'No, the mists are clearing and now I see it's... (the opposite).'

Step 4: Continue in this way, adding more and more detail.

Step 5: Now you're ready for a spectacular finish along the following lines. 'This person has an important message for you. Many times this person... has wanted to give you the message... but never felt able to... until now... but within the next forty-eight hours... a situation will occur... in which their message will be very useful to you... and as you think about this person... so you will begin to understand... what the message is...'.

———————————xxx———————————

So now you know how some of those seemingly impossible mind-reading feats are carried out. The last part of the exercise utilizes Ericksonian speech patterns, which we'll be learning a lot more about. If you find the exercise difficult, you can make it easier by switching from an invisible crystal ball to palm reading. The procedure is the same but this time you'll receive subtle 'Yes/No' signals unconsciously given by the subject through their hand.

The signals to watch for... and give

How did you get on with the calibration exercises? You should have learned a great deal about body language. Here are some of the things you should be taking note of and learning to match and mirror when appropriate.

VOICE

We all instinctively tend to modify our language to be more like that of the people we're with. In a group of people where expletives are used freely you might also pepper your language with them; in a different group you might be careful to avoid them.

Rapport also has to do with speed, volume and rhythm. As an exercise, first of all try matching fairly closely then switch to a different pattern – faster/slower, louder/softer – and see if the other person begins to follow you. This has a very practical application when someone is angry and shouting. You raise your voice a little but then steadily lower it, speaking slowly and calmly. The other person will probably follow.

NLP makes a great deal about primary representational systems, and the subject is certainly worth knowing about. NLP holds that when people process information they tend to favour one of three methods, and that's reflected in the way they speak:

- ▶ *they see visual images*
- ▶ *they hear sounds*
- ▶ *they experience feelings.*

For example, ask three people for their opinions about something. One might reply like this: 'The way I see the situation from my point of view is…'. The second might say: 'From what I hear, people are saying…'. And the last might reply: 'I feel this concept is difficult to grasp…'. The conclusion is that the first person tends to process information *visually*, the second is more orientated towards *sound*, while the third thinks in terms of *feelings*.

If you notice that someone leans heavily towards one system or another then it's worth following suit to tune in and establish rapport. But most people jumble up all three (just like the last sentence did) and there are other things far more important in terms of getting along with people.

Of course, the most significant aspect of your voice is what you actually say. It will be very hard to establish rapport with someone if you despise their opinions and they despise yours. If rapport is the most important thing then you may have to pretend, or at least avoid subjects you suspect will be controversial. It's also vital to acknowledge other people's problems and fears. Never ignore them or brush them aside. A simple formula, if you find it difficult to show a genuine interest, is to more or less repeat back to them what they've said to you. In other words, if someone tells you their mother has a health problem then you say, 'I'm so sorry to hear your mother has been ill'. Also try switching into second position, that is, seeing the situation through the other person's eyes (to remind yourself about multiple perspectives turn to Chapter 2).

POSTURE AND MANNERISMS

Let's say you're interviewing people for a job. Through a peephole you can see into the waiting room. Spying on the candidates in this way you see:

▶ *a woman drumming her fingers on the arm of her chair*
▶ *a man, legs crossed, swinging one leg backwards and forwards*
▶ *a man, chin on hand, constantly shifting his gaze from one candidate to another and to every part of the room*
▶ *a woman sitting right on the edge of her chair, hands clasped on her lap, leaning slightly forwards*
▶ *a man with his legs out full length in front of him, leaning back with his hands behind his head.*

These are all communications: 'I feel tense'; 'I'm wound up'; 'I'm bored and in need of stimulation'; 'I'm up for this'; 'I really don't care and therefore I'm very relaxed'.

In fact, most human communication is non-verbal. Probably about 80 per cent. That might surprise you. But just think about it for a moment. What are your feelings about men with shaven heads?

Or long hair? Or earrings? Or men or women with tattoos? Wearing kaftans? Green wellies? Chewing gum?

These are all things that are liable to cause some reaction in you. You have been communicated with. Whether or not you accurately decode the communication is another matter – but communication it is. And to establish rapport, all you have to do is copy.

Don't be in any way obvious, of course. If the other person even suspects anything, they'll think you're weird or making fun of them. The matching and mirroring has to be extremely subtle, just as it is when it's natural. The difference is that you're doing it on purpose, either to accelerate rapport or to create rapport with someone you normally wouldn't get on with.

Insight

Don't rush to match or mirror someone. You don't have to make a movement immediately the other person does. There can be a lapse of a few seconds or even more.

You can also deliberately break rapport, perhaps to bring a conversation to an end. Sucking air in through the teeth and raising the shoulders, as if to stand up, is a standard signal. Looking away and giving a shrug is another. Or you might abruptly change the tempo to a rapid 'winding-up' speed.

HAVE A GO

▶ Look around in any large, crowded waiting area – such as an airport lounge – and try to identify those people who are alone, those who are with people they don't know very well, those who have been together a long time, and those whose matching and mirroring suggests they are actively engaged in getting on fairly intimate terms.

▶ Check your skills by first of all matching and mirroring for a while and then switching to a new behaviour to see if the other person copies you. If you've truly established rapport they should.

EYES

The meaning of eye movements is one of the most controversial aspects of NLP. The safest thing that can be said is that *some* people move their eyes in specific ways, according to the nature of the information they're processing. For example, lots of us raise our eyes heavenwards when someone surprises us with a tricky, embarrassing or (what appears to us) stupid question. But NLP goes a lot further.

Here is the standard NLP model for a right-handed person (for some left-handed people the pattern, it is said, may be reversed):

- *Eyes up to their left: they're recalling something they've seen.*
- *Eyes up to their right: they're visualizing something they've never actually seen.*
- *Eyes horizontally across to their left: they're recalling a sound.*
- *Eyes horizontally across to their right: they're making up a sound (composing music, for example).*
- *Eyes down to their left: they're talking internally to themselves.*
- *Eyes down to their right: they're recalling a feeling.*

If you'd like to test this out and come to your own conclusions then get some friends to be guinea pigs and ask questions designed to elicit the six different eye movements. For example, for visual recall, you might ask, 'Describe the view from your bedroom window', while for a feeling you might ask, 'Describe the sensation of diving into cold water'.

If you can identify these or other consistent eye patterns in a particular individual then you have a useful tool. On the basis of the NLP model, for example, if you asked somebody to describe where they were last night and you noted that their eyes flicked up to their right then you'd know they were making the whole thing up. However, various scientists have disputed that this pattern is common – let alone universal.

A very much more proven eye phenomenon is that of pupil size. Of course, pupils adapt to the light (and can be affected by drugs), but assuming stable lighting conditions, then dilation (enlargement) indicates pleasure. There's even a science known as 'pupillometrics', a term first used in 1975 by Eckhard Hess, a biopsychologist at the University of Chicago.

Most famously, the pupils of both men and women dilate when they're sexually attracted to someone. And, intriguingly, that dilation is itself attractive to the other person. In one study, men were shown pairs of photographs of various women: one with normal pupils, the other identical except that the pupil size had been enlarged. The men said they found the images with dilated pupils more attractive, although they were unable to explain why. Women also find men with dilated pupils more attractive, especially when (according to a study at Edinburgh University) they're ovulating.

Controlling your own pupil dilation artificially isn't easy. If you're not attracted by someone else or deriving much pleasure from their company you could try thinking of something that does give you pleasure – pupils also dilate for good food, pets, landscapes and (in the case of women) babies.

BREATHING

John Grinder says he knew when he'd secured the interest of Milton Erickson by his breathing. Breathing is one of those things that most people only notice unconsciously, but many animals are highly attuned to it. If you've done much riding you'll know that holding your breath is a good way to make a horse feel nervous. Sucking air in through the teeth and snorting air out down the nose are other signs of tension, while breathing out in an exaggerated way, perhaps with the tongue showing, indicates an abrupt release of tension.

You can usually see when a person is breathing in and out by the rise and fall of the shoulders or chest and sometimes by the narrowing and flaring of the nostrils. Simply follow the same breathing pattern for rapport.

CONGRUENCE AND LIES

When well-balanced people are behaving naturally, they're congruent. That's to say, everything about them is harmonious. Every aspect of body language is in alignment and reflects their beliefs and values. But when somebody deliberately sets out to mislead or manipulate then – almost inevitably – there will be a degree of incongruence. One aspect of body language will contradict another. That's something you'll be looking for.

Unless they're very practised, people who are lying tend to exhibit signs of tension such as sweating, twitching and abnormal voice patterns with odd changes of tone and speed. In order to try to conceal the tension, people who are lying may hold themselves very still. Other signs may be very personal to the individual so your calibration skills will need to be good.

If you pretend you believe the lies you'll probably get on fairly well, especially if the other person believes their own lies. But you'll simply be tricking one another, which isn't true rapport. That would come from making it clear you like the person *behind* the lies.

Just as you're watching other people for signs of incongruence, so they'll be watching for it in you. They probably won't be doing it consciously, but at the unconscious level, they'll be aware when things 'don't feel right'. When you're using the techniques in this chapter to be more persuasive it's important that you remain congruent. This adaptation of the New Behaviour Generator will help.

HAVE A GO
Step 1: You are the director of a movie in which you are also the star. As the director, give instructions to yourself about the body language you should exhibit if you are to seem congruent.

Watch yourself being congruent as you interact with other people. In your role as director, make any corrections or changes you think necessary.

Step 2: Once you're satisfied, step into the movie and experience what it's like to feel congruent, as seen through your own eyes as the star. Not only see but hear everything you're saying to be persuasive and feel what it's like. (In other words, you've now switched from third position to first position, from dissociation to association – if you've forgotten about multiple perspectives, refer to Chapter 2.) Note the reaction of other people. Is it what you want it to be? Also check that this new behaviour really is suitable for you.

Step 3: If you're not happy with anything, return to your role as director, make the necessary changes and repeat Step 2.

DEALING WITH INATTENTION

People who are paying attention tend to be fairly still and ignore distractions. They lean forwards – perhaps with their heads slightly tilted – and gaze steadily with reduced blinking and maybe a furrowed brow. If they're open to what's being said their bodies are open (see below) and they may nod and make encouraging noises. It's easy to get in rapport with them. On the other hand, people who aren't interested tend to fidget, get distracted easily, look around for more interesting diversions and lean back. How you deal with that depends to a large extent on the context. A schoolmaster of mine used to throw pieces of chalk at pupils who had glazed over. More subtle devices include sudden changes of volume and rhythm and more energetic movements.

DEALING WITH CLOSED ATTITUDES

When people are open to others, to information and to experiences they literally tend to have 'open bodies'. That's to say, their hands will be open and their arms and legs will not be crossed. Clothing may also be open: jacket off, tie undone, shirt or blouse open at the neck. Note, however, that an open body can also denote aggression – come and get me if you dare. A closed body is the reverse; hands making fists, arms and legs crossed, shoulders hunched, head tucked down, are all signs that someone is shutting the world out. (But always bear in mind that these are also normal reactions to cold.)

In order to influence other people, you need to be able to get them out of closed postures into open postures. One way is to ask them to do something that requires them to use their hands. As a salesman you could, for example, pass out sample products. Another technique is to match their body language while you try to establish rapport in other ways. Once you have a connection, you then lead them into more open postures by opening your posture. If you've successfully initiated rapport they should follow your lead.

SUBMISSION AND DOMINANCE

When someone is submissive the body is usually closed (see above), made as small as possible, and kept still, with the head down. In this mood people tend to smile a lot with the mouth but not with the eyes, which will be wide. Hands are often open, palms up, to show that there is no weapon. Movement is slow but jerky and there may be signs of tension such as sweating, a white face, pulling the hair and face touching.

By contrast, people who are feeling dominant make their bodies bigger, by pulling themselves up to their full height with arms held out and legs apart – which, by exposing the groin, is also a way for men to say 'mine is bigger than yours'. They may demonstrate their superiority by showing off expensive accessories (watches, cuff links, jewellery and so on), by 'invading' the territory of other people (getting very close, putting feet on the furniture) and interrupting or speaking over them. Dominant people tend not to worry about showing disapproval in their facial expressions.

Who dominates is something that tends to be established at the outset of a meeting. In the handshake, the dominant person aims to get his or her hand on top – not at the side – and will follow up with an elbow hold or a shoulder hold. They may either stare for a long time or, alternatively, quickly 'cut' the other person. Dominant people often use long silences when speaking, during which they look around at the people listening or stare off into space as they visualize their own importance.

You can rub along with dominant people simply by doing what they want – but that isn't the same as rapport. Indeed, it may be that rapport isn't actually possible. If you want to go for it, you'll simply have to rise to the challenge and match them.

ROMANCE

It's not only birds and animals that preen and display. Humans do it too. Tossing the head, running fingers through hair, thrusting out breasts, holding in the stomach and holding out the arms to make the shoulders look bigger are all examples. Eyes are vitally important. From a distance someone may look for longer than normal, then look away, then back again. Close up, the pupils will be seen to be dilated (see *Eyes* above) when someone feels attracted. Eyes will also tend to go where a person would like to touch – for example, the lips or the groin. Most women will have had the experience of looking into the faces of men whose eyes keep darting down to their cleavage. People may unconsciously caress themselves in the way they'd like to caress the person they're interested in, or to be caressed by that person. The signal may also be given consciously. As rapport begins to develop, so people will automatically match one another – and again, this can be done consciously to try to create rapport.

NEGOTIATIONS

What happens when one team of people goes to negotiate with another team? Let's say the directors of company A and the directors of company B. Without thinking, the company A directors will all sit on one side of the table and the company B directors will all sit on the opposite side. To most of us this feels so normal that we don't question it. But is it a good idea? It immediately creates an 'us and them' atmosphere. Sometimes that might be what you want but, for the purposes of conciliation, compromise and finding a win–win solution, it would actually be far better for 'opposite numbers' to sit next to one another. Thus the managing directors could sit side by side, the finance directors could sit side by side, and so on.

The Milton Model in everyday life

Largely by a process of observation, and by trial and error, Milton Erickson pioneered the techniques that were later modelled by Grinder and Bandler. Those techniques have now been studied and emulated by hypnotists and therapists all over the world. But many of them can also be used in everyday life and it's those we're going to look at here.

These everyday techniques are sometimes known as 'conversational hypnosis' because, when he employed them, all Erickson appeared to do was chat with clients and tell rambling, oddly paced, stories – the point of which wasn't always apparent.

Milton Erickson was quite capable of interfering very directly in people's lives when he thought it best, but his normal approach – the Milton Model approach – was to help people work out the answers for themselves. Erickson believed that the unconscious mind was always alert and therefore always accessible but that it couldn't be given direct instructions. That's why simply telling someone to give up smoking or drinking is almost completely ineffective.

Instead, he would be deliberately vague – 'artfully vague' Bandler and Grinder called it – so his clients would have to *think*. People who have to work things out for themselves:

▶ *remember better than when someone else tells them*
▶ *believe in their conclusions more than in those they are told*

- *prefer the ideas that result over other people's, because they are their own*
- *use a so-called 'transderivational' search (TDS) of the unconscious mind, which can result in changes at a deep level*
- *are distracted while they're thinking, which can be an opportunity to plant a suggestion in the unconscious mind.*

If you're a very direct sort of person, you may find it hard to adopt the Milton Model. Indeed, there are times when precision – the very opposite of the Milton Model – is essential. But we're not concerned here with something like flying an aeroplane. We're talking about changing the way people think and feel. That change comes about more easily when people do it for themselves *from within*. Your role, then, is to prompt them into beginning that process. By making vague, confusing and ambiguous statements you force people to use their own minds to unravel the meaning. That process of discovery means that the ideas they develop are perceived as their own. And because the ideas are 'their own' they obviously cause no resistance.

USING QUESTIONS

Rather than giving instructions, which might meet with resistance, you can often get a better result by asking a question. For example, you might ask, 'How far are you willing to go?' By posing that question, you make it harder for the other person to say anything less than 'all the way'. And once they've said 'all the way' then they're committed.

The power of questions was vividly illustrated in an experiment (Barber, Dalai and Calverley 1968) in which people who had been hypnotized were later asked one of two things. Of those asked, 'Did you experience the hypnotic state as basically *similar* to the waking state?' 83 per cent said they did. But of those asked, 'Did you experience the hypnotic state as basically *different* from the waking state?' 72 per cent said *they* did. In other words, merely posing the question changed people's perceptions of their experiences.

See if you can find a way of rephrasing the following instruction as a question that might have a better chance of getting the result you want:

> 'Give up smoking.'

Don't look at my examples until you've come up with at least one question. Okay? Well, you could ask something like:

> 'Do you think it's possible for a strong-willed person to give up smoking just like that?'

> 'How much better do you think you would you feel if you gave up smoking?'

> 'What would you do with the extra 21 years of life that half of all smokers miss out on?'

No one is suggesting that the asking of such questions will immediately make anyone give up smoking, but the ideas planted will continue to work on the unconscious in a way that direct instructions do not.

USING NEGATIVES AND POSITIVES

When people are feeling uncertain about something, it's important for rapport to show that you understand their negative feelings:

> 'I understand how you feel.'

> 'Everyone finds it difficult the first time.'

In fact, you can simply repeat back to people the negative things they've said: 'So you're saying you feel you're not ready to take this step...'. You can then overcome resistance by introducing negatives to discharge their feelings. For example, you might say:

> 'You don't have to continue if you're not enjoying it.'

'You won't have to sign anything.'

'You don't have to make a decision until you're completely convinced.'

Negatives, then, can be useful in certain situations. They can diffuse resistance. But when giving instructions, it's generally a very bad idea to phrase them in negative terms. Let's say, for example, that you're skiing or snowboarding with a group of beginners and you call out, 'Don't go near the edge of the path'. Your friends will then focus on the drop at the side and repeat the mantra 'Don't go near the edge, don't go near the edge...'. And they'll find their skis or snowboards inexorably headed towards the chasm, as if pulled there by some unseen force. In actual fact, they are pulled by a force – the force of their own unconscious minds. By focusing on the edge, they orientate their bodies towards it and their unconscious minds, having been given the keyword 'edge', ensure that they get there. The correct course is to make sure your beginners focus on staying on the path by giving a *positive* instruction: 'Do stay in the middle of the path, do stay in the middle of the path...'. So here's a very important lesson:

Always give instructions in positive terms.

Insight

It's important to give people an experience of success. Because once they have that experience they know how to repeat it.

HAVE A GO

Find a way of rephrasing these negative statements in positive terms without changing the meaning:

▶ *'Don't ski over the edge of the path.'*
▶ *'Don't spill any of this.'*
▶ *'You'll never get better if you keep thinking negative thoughts.'*
▶ *'You'll fail the exam if you spend more than twenty minutes on each question.'*

Now add in what you've learned about the power of questions by rephrasing your positive statements as questions.

CAUSE AND EFFECT

We're all used to statements which link a cause and an effect. You might say, for example: 'Prices are going up next month so it would be a good idea to order now'. The fact is, we're so used to them that any compound statement that begins with something obviously true tends to make us feel that the second part will also be right. The truth of the first part rubs off on the second:

> *'It's an unusually beautiful day so let's go to the beach.'*

Put like that it seems such a natural thing to do (even if you should be at work). A variation is what's known as 'implication' using an 'if' construction:

> *'If you sit in that chair you'll feel more relaxed.'*

The person who sits in the chair will generally follow their first positive response (sitting in the chair) with the second.

HAVE A GO
See if you can create some compound statements for the following circumstances. Remember, the first part of your sentence has to be something that's obviously right. The second part – your real aim – should appear to be a logical consequence, even though it may not be.

- ▶ *You want someone to donate money to charity.*
- ▶ *You would like a raise at work.*
- ▶ *You want someone to accept a lower price for something.*

PACING AND LEADING

Pacing and leading together form a powerful technique in hypnosis but can also be used effectively on people in their normal waking state. Essentially, you feed their experience back to them (pacing) and once you've established rapport, you then guide them in the direction you want to go (leading). If you watch mentalists like Derren Brown and hypnotists like Paul McKenna on TV or YouTube you'll see them using this technique a lot.

Pacing can be:

▶ *Physical – you match the other person's posture, mannerisms, tone of voice, breathing and so on.*
▶ *Verbal – you tell the other person the things they're experiencing at that moment.*

This pacing not only creates rapport but also establishes a positive momentum which the other person may find hard to resist. Let's hear a good salesman in action: 'You have a very nice car there. It's a recent model with only 20,000 miles on the clock, and silver is a popular colour so in part-exchange I can offer you...'. The customer knows everything the salesman has said is true. It *is* a nice car, it *is* a recent model, it *is* low mileage and it *is* silver. So when the salesman makes a low offer the customer, carried along by the momentum, is inclined to accept.

HAVE A GO
Today, try feeding people's experiences back to them before going on to make a request and see if it makes a difference. (Tip: don't make it too obvious.)

PRESUPPOSITIONS AND BINDS

The idea of presuppositions and binds is to make it necessary for the other person to summon up a certain strength of will to resist you. If they don't have that mental strength then you will persuade them.

Let's look at some simple presuppositions:

▶ *'Would you like to pay by credit card?'*
▶ *'You've definitely chosen the best one.'*
▶ *'You're so right to go for the pink.'*

If these are said *before* any buying decision has actually been made then they have the effect of bumping the customer into doing what you want. Essentially, you're *presupposing* that they've decided to buy and they now have to actively resist you if they want to get out of the purchase. Now let's have a look at something more sophisticated:

> *'Would you like to do this now or would you like to do it in an hour?'*

This presupposes that the person would like to do it *at all*. He or she now has to, as it were, overturn the presumption ('Neither') or opt for one of them. For that reason, this type of presumption is also known as a 'bind' because it puts the other person in the artificial position of having to choose between two things when, in reality, the range of choices may be much larger. Quite often, the other person won't even notice that their options have been restricted.

> *'Would you like to do this now or would you prefer to do it in an hour?'*

This is similar to the previous presupposition but now, by using the word 'prefer' and marking it with a slight emphasis, you are guiding the other person towards doing it in an hour, rather than now.

> *'We're going to have to choose between two courses of action.'*

This presupposes that there *are* only two possibilities (both of which are favourable to you) and tends to prevent anyone coming up with a third or fourth (that might not be favourable to you).

> *'You've done incredibly well, so you're not going to have any problem with the next step.'*

This presupposes the person has already agreed to the next step.

STORIES AND QUOTES

It was probably his use of stories that was Erickson's most distinctive skill. People would come to him with a problem and, instead of doing anything about it (or so it appeared), he'd tell them a story. A few days or weeks later the problem would be gone.

Rather than say 'Do this' or 'Don't do that' (although he was also quite capable of giving orders when appropriate), Erickson would instead plant seeds that would sprout inside his clients' minds. The whole point of using stories, of course, is to go directly to the unconscious and bypass the resistance of the conscious mind. So the stories can't be too obvious.

Erickson's clients would usually be in trance when they heard his stories and, as a result, they would become heightened in their significance. But even with someone in a 'normal waking state' the skilful use of stories can have powerful results.

Suitable stories:

- *entertain and capture the other person's attention*
- *bypass resistance because they are non-threatening*
- *allow the other person to deduce the meaning*
- *carry on 'working' indefinitely*
- *are less likely to be forgotten than straightforward statements.*

If you've always been a fairly direct person, initially you'll struggle to come up with anecdotes that suit the circumstances. But if you work at it, over time you can build up your own personal 'library' and have an anecdote for every occasion. It will help if you think in terms of universal experiences, which could apply to just about everybody.

Erickson was the master of this technique. When a woman consulted him about tinnitus he told her a story about the time he slept on the floor of a noisy factory and how at first he couldn't make out anything anyone said and yet, in the morning, he could hear everyone clearly because his mind had, as it were, turned down the factory sounds. The point of the story was, of course, that the woman could similarly learn to turn down the ringing of the tinnitus. Similarly, in the case of a woman with severe nerve pain, Erickson spoke about the way a labourer would get calluses on his hands. He thus planted the idea that an overused nerve might also develop a similar insensitivity. In both these cases, the clients were willing and in trance and it didn't matter that the stories were fairly obvious. But if you're dealing with, say, a rebellious teenager, your stories will need to be more subtle.

Let's look at a practical application. Your teenage son won't study. So you concoct a little story which you tell to your partner, knowing that your difficult teenager is within hearing:

> *'I bumped into Joe Brown today. He's really concerned about his son Harry because, apparently, he's a magnet for the girls. It seems they all want to go out with someone who's got good prospects. He gets top marks in everything and the girls like that...'*

And so on. You could lower your voice now and then to make it clear you don't want to be overheard. The unconscious usually pays attention to lowered voices.

Insight

In dealing with a situation in which resistance is almost inevitable (for example, when talking to your own children), it's generally better not to make yourself the subject of the story, but to talk about someone else. It can help to use quotes. For example, you might say: 'A very wealthy man once told me, "Money never made me happier..."'.

If you're not convinced by the power of stories, think back to the things that have shaped your own outlook. For example, what about the story of Robin Hood, who stole from the rich to give to the poor? Did that mould your views in any way? Or maybe real life stories of heroism or success or sacrifice? And, of course, the parables told by Jesus have had an immense effect on Western culture. There are whole books of Erickson's stories (see *Taking It Further*) and, as a starting point, you might like to borrow them. Here's a taste to inspire you.

GETTING MOTIVATED TO LEARN

Erickson would talk about the way all infants eventually learn to walk, never giving up, despite the complexity of coordinating the muscles to be able to balance and move. Or he would tell stories about the way infants laboriously learn the alphabet and how to read and write.

TRUSTING THE UNCONSCIOUS

Erickson had a story about being unable to speak until he was four years old. However, his sister who was two years younger was already talking, '...and she is still talking but she hasn't said anything'. Erickson's mother was unconcerned, believing he would talk 'when the time arrived'. The point of the story was that the unconscious can be trusted to provide the appropriate response at the right time.

On other occasions Erickson would tell how as a young man he sold books to pay his way through college. One day, while trying to persuade a farmer to buy, the young Erickson *unconsciously* began scratching the backs of the farmer's pigs. The farmer, who had previously ruled out buying anything, was so pleased that he changed his mind: 'You like hogs', he said. 'You know how to scratch 'em the way they like to be scratched'.

A third story concerned a college student who correctly predicted the ten questions that would be set in the final exam by noting the special intonation the lecturer gave to the subjects he considered the most important.

ESTABLISHING RAPPORT

The story about the pigs (above) is also a story about establishing rapport. Erickson did things the way the farmer liked.

EXPANDING HORIZONS

Erickson would ask clients to describe all the ways of moving from the room they were in to the adjacent room. The clients would come up with various methods such as walking, jumping, hopping, skipping and so on, but Erickson would always be able to find additional ones the client hadn't thought of, such as walking backwards or going to the airport, flying round the world, returning to the house, entering by the back door and thereby gaining access to the room. The point, of course, was to show that you can always find another way of doing things when you think creatively.

ADDICTION

Erickson was consulted by an alcoholic whose parents and grandparents were also alcoholics. Erickson instructed him to go to the Botanical Gardens and '...marvel at cacti that can survive three years without water, without rain – and do a lot of thinking'. The suggestion worked, as confirmed many years later by the man's daughter.

PHRASING

The pace at which you speak – and the way you separate groups of words by pauses – are crucial to your powers of persuasion. Most of us speak too quickly. If you think of the politicians whose words you give weight to (even if you don't necessarily agree), they'll probably be people who speak slowly and use plenty of pauses. Barack Obama immediately comes to mind. As we saw above, long pauses are a signal of dominance. And words delivered slowly give the impression of being well-considered and important, even if they're not. But there's another aspect to phrasing and that's its hypnotic effect. When you're up close to someone, attuning your speech to the rhythm of their breathing can be very powerful.

Compare this sentence with the first sentence of the above paragraph, for example:

> *The pace... at which you speak... and the way... you separate... groups of words... by pauses... are crucial... to your powers... of persuasion.*

Do you see the difference?

HAVE A GO
Ask a friend to help you. Try speaking to him or her in this new way. And ask your friend to speak to you in the same way. Then discuss the effects.

Motivation direction

We've already encountered motivation direction in Chapter 5, as it applies to you. It's what's known in NLP as a meta program and it applies equally to other people. Just to remind you, motivation direction is another way of saying 'stick or carrot'. Some people seem to respond more to sticks and some people more to carrots. NLP looks at this in terms of being motivated *away* from things that are negative and unpleasant, or being motivated *towards* things that are rewarding and enjoyable.

If you want to encourage somebody, you need to know their motivation direction. Generally speaking:

▶ *'Towards' people are fired up by goals and plans for the future and tend to be ambitious, energetic and optimistic. You motivate them using words such as: achieve, target, drive, reach, top and summit.*

▶ *'Away from' people tend to be more aware of possible problems and are therefore more cautious. You motivate them using words such as: avoid, overcome, prevent, bunker and trap.*

Using amnesia

Amnesia is a rather frightening word but, in fact, it simply means a loss of memory. Most people associate it with the word 'total' which, fortunately, is rare. Partial amnesia, on the other hand, is common.

Probably you've had the experience of someone suggesting an idea to you that, in fact, you had suggested to them a week or more previously. However much you protest, they insist it's their idea and say they have no memory of you ever having said any such thing. That's the frustrating side of partial amnesia. But you can also make the phenomenon work in your favour when you deliberately plant an idea that you *hope* another person will enthusiastically adopt as their own.

Partial amnesia can also work to your advantage when you don't want someone to think things over in case they change their mind or develop a resistance later.

Here, then, is a way of encouraging partial amnesia. Change the subject the *instant* you've planted your idea and then to talk about the new subject quickly, at length and in detail. The planted idea will remain in the unconscious but may be forgotten by the conscious mind.

10 THINGS TO REMEMBER

1 *Consider the ethical implications before you use the Milton Model.*

2 *If you want to have a positive influence on people then you first have to establish rapport.*

3 *Matching and mirroring are powerful techniques for establishing rapport.*

4 *Calibrating means observing body language and relating it to a person's emotions; it calls for the development of good sensory acuity.*

5 *You can improve your sensory acuity through the exercises in this chapter.*

6 *About 80 per cent of human communication is through body language.*

7 *The Milton Model is based on the 'artfully vague' techniques of the hypnotherapist Milton Erickson.*

8 *By using a bind, you can present someone else with a limited range of choices – all of them to your advantage.*

9 *`Stories can often influence people far more powerfully than direct statements.*

10 *Speaking slowly with pauses timed to the rhythm of breathing can give greater weight to the things you say.*

HOW AM I GETTING ON?

▶ *Have you worked through the various exercises for developing sensory acuity?*

▶ *Have you identified the body language that goes with 'Yes' and the body language that goes with 'No' in at least one other person?*

▶ *Have you deliberately matched and mirrored another person without them consciously realizing?*

▶ *Have you paced someone and then successfully led them?*

▶ *Have you stopped yourself saying what you were about to say and, instead, rephrased your comments as a question?*

▶ *Have you used a presupposition or bind on someone?*

▶ *Have you told someone a story instead of giving an instruction?*

▶ *Have you tried coordinating your speech with the rhythm of the person you're speaking to?*

▶ *Have you worked out the motivation direction of those close to you at home or at work?*

▶ *Have you been able to induce amnesia in anybody?*

The techniques described in this chapter can't be perfected in a few hours, but aim to answer 'Yes' to at least six of the above questions within two weeks. You'll need to practise daily to get the techniques right. While you're doing so, keep in mind the following NLP presuppositions:

> **The meaning of your communication is the response you get. If what you are doing isn't working, do something else.**

8

Transform your love life

In this chapter you will learn:
- *how you and your partner can be the stars of a romantic movie*
- *how you can recapture the romance of those early days*
- *how you can avoid rows or quickly get over them*
- *how you can develop more confidence and skill in lovemaking*
- *how to get over a break-up.*

> *Underlying every behaviour is a positive intention.*
>
> NLP presupposition

Are you in love? Do you want to stay in love? Do you want to fall back in love? Do you want to increase the love you feel? Do you want to be a better lover? NLP can help you achieve all of these things.

How to increase those loving feelings

Can you remember when you first met your partner? When you first began to get a special feeling? When you had your first kiss? When you first made love? When you made your first trip together? When you first moved in together?

When you think back on it, it's a movie, isn't it! A romantic story. Well, rather than watch television, why not lay back and, inside your head, run the movie in which *you* are one of the stars and *your partner* is the other! Let's call it *Love Story*. When you've finished watching it, feelings of love will overwhelm you.

HAVE A GO
Step 1: Select five very different romantic scenes from your life together with your partner.

Step 2: Acting like a film director, consider what qualities ('submodalities') you could change to maximize the romantic impact of each scene. There are all kinds of possibilities. For example, you can use several cameras from different viewpoints – or in NLP jargon, different 'perceptual positions'. You can show things through your own eyes at the time (first position), as well as through your partner's eyes (second position). And you can have yet another camera showing how you both would have looked to an observer (third position). Why not a slow motion sequence with some romantic music? How about a close-up for that first kiss? Maybe some soft-focus and low, mood lighting? And, of course, a bedroom scene. Nowadays, every romantic film has a bedroom scene. (We'll be having a look at that subject in more detail.)

Step 3: Once you're satisfied with your five scenes, run them one after the other to make your movie. Then run them all again a little faster. Then faster still.

Step 4: By now you should be overwhelmed by warm and loving feelings for your partner. Go and share them.

———————————— xxx ————————————

Running your very own romantic movie is something you should do regularly. Make a point of it at least once a week and your love will intensify.

To keep it interesting, vary the direction and as time moves on, you can add new scenes.

The Circle of Love

No matter how much you express your love for your partner, you can always express more. It's not just a case of what you *say* from time to time. Nor what you occasionally *give*. Nor what you *do* now and then. It's a question of feeling and radiating your love all the time you're together. This technique, which I call the Circle of Love, works on the same principles as the Circle of Confidence, with which you're already familiar.

Step 1: Search your memory for a past situation in which you felt overwhelmed by love. Relive that loving time, seeing and hearing everything in as much detail as possible. Particularly notice how you looked and how the love was oozing out of you. Accentuate the submodalities associated with love. Spin the feeling up.

Step 2: Imagine a circle on the floor. Take the love you felt on that previous occasion and pour it into the circle. Immediately the circle takes on a colour – the colour that, to you, is the colour of love. Maybe there's romantic music, too.

Step 3: Are there any other qualities you'll need? Maybe tenderness? Maybe empathy? If so, repeat the procedure, also pouring those qualities into your circle.

Step 4: Turn your thoughts to all those future occasions when you'll be wanting to feel those qualities. Select a cue. For example, it could simply be your partner arriving or it could be waking up next to him or her.

Step 5: Holding that cue in your mind, step into the circle and visualize all those qualities rising up from the floor, permeating you and being radiated by you.

Step 6: Future pace. Visualize the future unfolding from that cue moment. See yourself behaving with love and all the other qualities you've selected for your Circle of Love.

When the cue moment arrives for real, visualize the circle on the floor and step into it. Now express all that love to your partner.

The way we were

Sometimes it's a case of gradually drifting apart over months or years. And then there comes a point when you think of the way you *were* and want to get back to it once more.

By now you should be very familiar with the Swish concept – in effect, creating an emotion with one image and then quickly substituting a new image which acquires the same emotional charge as the first. Here we're going to use it to reawaken the feelings you used to have but which have now, perhaps, grown stale.

For the following Swish exercise, find yourself somewhere comfortable and quiet.

Step 1: Think of a time when you and your partner were deliriously happy together. From that period, select an image of your partner that made you overflow with love.

Step 2: Utterly revel in those loving feelings. Increase all the submodalities associated with love. Spin the feeling up to its maximum: see, hear, touch, taste and smell everything.

Step 3: Call up an image of your partner today and immediately Swish it into the place of the previous image, while retaining all the submodalities of the previous image and all the emotions.

Step 4: Repeat Steps 1–3 as many times as necessary, until those same loving feelings from years ago are firmly attached to your image of your partner today.

Modelling other couples

Sometimes you just can't seem to find the answers, either inside yourself or together with your partner. Then maybe it's the moment to see how other couples handle things – in other words, to do some modelling. If you've forgotten about modelling, refer back to Chapter 3.

Of course, it's virtually impossible to know everything about the way another two people behave together. But that doesn't rule out modelling as a useful technique in your love life. In fact, you almost certainly have been modelling, whether you realize it or not. For example, you would have modelled the way your parents related to one another when you were growing up. Or the way a step-parent related to one of your parents.

What you then did with your model was up to you. You may have copied it unconsciously. Or you may have quite consciously behaved in the opposite way. But, for most of us, it's our parents' relationship that's our starting point.

As an adult, you can now choose who you model. Do you know anyone whose love life you admire? Think very carefully. Men have a tendency to focus on the skills of womanizers, but having a large number of relationships is failure, not success.

Try to spend some time with that person and his or her partner. As usual in modelling, don't ask any questions at first. Just absorb the way they interact. The things they say and don't say. The gestures they make and don't make. Their ways of dealing with potential conflict.

Once you've absorbed their way of being, ask yourself these kinds of questions:

▶ *Are they as happy together as I thought?*
▶ *How many hours a day are they happy together?*

- *How often do they make one another unhappy?*
- *What's the balance between happiness and unhappiness in this relationship?*
- *What do they do that's different?*
- *What should I copy?*
- *What could I do better?*
- *How much more happiness could I create in my relationship?*

Later ask *them* questions, such as:

- *What techniques do you use to maintain your love?*
- *How much time do you want to be a) together, b) with friends and c) on your own?*
- *How important is it to express your love verbally and physically?*
- *How do you deal with conflict?*

Hopefully they'll be open and truthful. Of course, what works for one couple may not work for you. But there are always useful lessons to be learned.

The subtraction part of the modelling process poses potential difficulties. Your partner will almost certainly become confused and upset if your behaviour is subject to sudden and seemingly erratic changes. This is a process, therefore, that you can only do *together*.

Dealing with rows

So you've had a row. The first thing you should do is recall the relevant NLP presupposition:

> *Underlying every behaviour is a positive intention.*

Whatever it was you were arguing about, your partner had a positive intention in view and it would help to find out what that was.

When there's been a row, many people sulk and spontaneously use an NLP technique without knowing it – but to make the situation worse, not better. What a lot of us do is think of all the previous occasions when our partners have also done things that have upset us. We link them all together in a continuous movie and just make ourselves feel more and more resentful and annoyed. That's a very bad idea if you want the relationship to move forwards (but it's a very good idea when a relationship actually does end – see *Breaking up is not so hard to do*). Far better is to use the *Love Story* technique described above and run a 'movie' of all the good times.

Insight

If you're really angry, you might not even be in the mood to think about the nice times. So I recommend writing down those wonderful scenes *right now*. Use a piece of card and put it somewhere safe in your wallet or bag where you can easily retrieve it. When you've had a row, take out that card and read through it, doing your best to visualize those nice times as vividly as possible.

USING DIFFERENT PERSPECTIVES

When there's a disagreement, everyone's immediate reaction is to see a situation from their own point of view. That's perfectly normal. But you should never leave it at that. Always change perspective (see Chapter 2). In other words, imagine entering into your partner's body (second position) and seeing the situation from his or her perspective. Empathize; try to feel what he or she is feeling.

Next try third position. That's to say, imagine standing back from the pair of you so you can see not only your partner but also yourself. How do you look? Unreasonable, perhaps? Maybe slightly ridiculous? Even funny? If you were a third person, what would you do? Perhaps say, 'Come on you two, kiss and make up.'

RE-ESTABLISHING RAPPORT

After a row, you often seem to lose all rapport with your partner. Somehow you no longer seem able to tune in to one another's thoughts. Your movements are no longer synchronized. There's no symmetry. Everything jars. The complicity has gone.

One of the things you can do to help is deliberately use the matching and mirroring described in the previous chapter. Since your partner knows you very well it will have to be extremely subtle. On the other hand, if your partner notices then that just might be the moment to have a good laugh together.

Insight

Some people think rows are good for 'clearing the air' and are a sign of passion. But you can 'clear the air' without having a row. It should be fairly obvious that you get good at what you practise. The more you row, the more you row. So try not to row. Instead, discuss differences of opinion calmly and with respect for your partner's views.

The Romantic Behaviour Generator

Do you always behave with your partner exactly as you would wish? Of course you don't. That's asking the impossible – but this adaptation of the New Behaviour Generator described in Chapter 5 can help.

HAVE A GO

This is an excellent way of installing a new behaviour. It can be used for everything – from being more empathetic to new lovemaking techniques. In this example, let's say you'd like to behave differently when criticized. At the moment your reaction is to withdraw love while you lick your wounds and think things over. You realize this makes the situation far worse then it need be, but you find it hard to change.

Step 1: Identify the old behaviour you would like to alter. In this example it's sulking.

Step 2: Identify the new behaviour you would like to have. For example, discussing the issue with good humour and without taking offence, so you both feel better afterwards.

Step 3: You are the director of a movie in which you are also the star. As the director, give instructions to yourself about the way you should behave. Watch yourself exhibit the new behaviour. In your role as director, make any corrections or changes you think necessary.

Step 4: Once you're satisfied, step into the movie and experience what it's like to have this new way of behaving, as seen through your own eyes as the star. Not only see but, of course, hear everything and feel what it's like. (In other words, you've now switched from third position to first position, that's to say, from dissociation to association.) Note the reaction of your partner. Is it what you want it to be?

Step 5: Move to second position. That's to say, see the whole scenario from your partner's viewpoint. Is it what your partner would want?

Step 6: Also check that this new behaviour really is suitable for you.

Step 7: If you're not happy with anything, return to your role as director, make the necessary changes and repeat Steps 3–6.

Step 8: Use future pacing. Visualize a situation in the future where you will want to behave in this new way. Look for a cue that could be used to trigger the behaviour automatically. In this example, it might be your partner looking angry, shouting or being tearful. Imagine yourself seeing or hearing the cue and immediately adopting the new behaviour. Play this 'film' as often as necessary until the new behaviour feels natural.

Step 9: Use the new behaviour in a real situation.

Improving your sex life

Anchors, as we've seen, are a normal part of our everyday experience and that includes our love lives. In fact, anchors are so much taken for granted when it comes to romance and sex that most people would probably find it hard to accept that they *are* anchors.

Take candles, for example. Most people would say that they're romantic – and low light does cause pupil dilation (see the previous chapter) – but otherwise there's nothing innately sexy about them. Before electricity, candles were just as normal as light bulbs are today. Nor is there anything innately romantic about champagne, nor oysters. But if you arrive home tonight and find a table lit by candles, champagne in an ice bucket and a plate of oysters then you'll probably feel very romantic indeed.

Insight

Some fetishes are simply examples of anchors that have become so 'successful' the fetishist can't function at all without them. For example there are men (men are more prone to this than women) who can't become excited unless their lovers wear rubber or high heels or fishnets.

DISCOVERING YOUR PARTNER'S ANCHORS

In a moment we'll be looking at how to create anchors for romance and sex. But before you do, it would be a good idea to discover your partner's existing anchors. He or she is bound to have quite a few – some entirely predictable and others much more personal that you might not know about.

HAVE A GO

With your partner, make a little game of it; each of you write down ten things that make you feel romantic and ten that make you feel aroused. Take turns guessing what your partner's anchors are. The one who gets the most correct is the winner (and the prize is up to you).

ESTABLISHING NEW ANCHORS

In Chapter 5 we learned the NLP technique for setting anchors. When it comes to romance and sex, however, we can install them in a more natural way. As long as the same things are always followed by romance and (if you want) sex, then they will become anchors over time. The more often anchors are actually followed by romance (and sex), the more powerful they become. So it can be a good idea to have something of a routine. Not *everything* has to be routine, of course, just those certain elements.

Here are some suggestions:

- ▶ *Kinaesthetic: the warmth of a log fire, nibbling an ear lobe, breathing in an ear, gently biting a tongue or lip while kissing, massaging the scalp or shoulders...*
- ▶ *Visual: a wink, an eyebrow raised in a particular way, a tongue run around the lips, special bed linen, a certain short skirt, certain underwear, stockings, a naked body...*
- ▶ *Olfactory: particular types of incense, perfume or aftershave...*
- ▶ *Gustatory: asparagus, oysters, a bottle of wine or champagne – but it has to be something special if it's to be an anchor, and served in a special way...*
- ▶ *Auditory: special pet names used only on romantic occasions, 'naughty' words, particular music only played for romantic occasions...*

Insight

Music for romance and sex shouldn't be played at other times or it will lose its power as an anchor. It can be fun to hum snatches of 'your' music very quietly and unobtrusively. Quite probably, your partner will soon find himself or herself also humming the music or playing it in the imagination. That, in turn, will make your partner feel sexy, possibly without even realizing why.

ADDING EROGENOUS ZONES

Given that the human body is fairly well endowed with sexual triggers is there really any point in creating more? Well, yes – a little variety in lovemaking technique is always good. And anyway, it's fun.

Here, then, is a way you can add to your partner's erogenous zones (or augment one that already exists). In effect, you'll be creating kinaesthetic anchors. You can also use the same procedure on yourself.

Insight

Your partner might be rather wary of the whole idea of setting anchors to do with sexual response. In fact, anchors can't make anybody do anything against their will. To use the motoring analogy once again, moving your foot to the brake pedal when a brake light comes on in front of you is an automatic response but you always have the 'manual override'. Should the situation demand it, you can swerve and accelerate instead. So it is with 'sexual anchors' too.

HAVE A GO

Step 1: Identify the area you wish to 'erogenize'. It helps if it already has at least some special sensitivity.

Step 2: Stimulate your partner's most erogenous area until she or he is moderately excited.

Step 3: Stimulate the new area you wish to 'erogenize' with three caresses, slaps, scratches, nibbles or pinches (depending on what works best for that place).

Step 4: Immediately stimulate your partner's most erogenous zone again three times.

Step 5: Continue like this, alternating between the two areas, rhythmically stimulating each three times, until your partner reports that the new zone is beginning to generate sexual feelings.

---

xxx

The general tendency of lovers is either to go straight for the most erogenous zone or to work through the erogenous zones *in turn*, from the least to the most. It's because this technique *alternates* between the most erogenous area and a less erogenous area (or areas) that it has its special effect. In fact, over a lengthy session it's possible to erogenize the entire body in this way, at least for a while.

Insight

Initially the kinaesthetic anchor works purely on the psychological level and because of that it can be installed quite quickly. However, if you continue with this stimulation each time you make love, then a genuine physiological response may eventually develop, as blood supply increases and nerve endings proliferate.

You can increase the effect by asking your partner to Swish images at the appropriate moments, first of all visualizing the most erogenous area and then abruptly substituting a visualization of the new area. The feelings associated with the first area will then become associated with the second.

DEALING WITH PERFORMANCE ANXIETY

Anxiety about sexual performance is fairly normal at the beginning of a relationship, but it can crop up at any time. When it does it can be fairly devastating because anxiety automatically leads to a reduction in blood flow where it's needed. Women can at least disguise it, but for men the effect is all too obvious. When you have a problem of this nature it's always best to discuss it with your partner. However, we'll assume here that you're tackling this on your own, at least for the moment. A simple visualization can help.

HAVE A GO
Step 1: In your mind's eye, see your partner preparing to have sex with you.

Step 2: Visualize the scene unfolding *very slowly*. Imagine yourself being completely relaxed as you see, hear, touch, taste and smell everything. See your partner becoming more and more aroused and see yourself responding just as you would wish to. Don't let any negative thoughts or doubts enter your mind while you're doing this.

Step 3: Adjust the submodalities to increase the impact. For example, you could zoom in on the details you find the most exciting or create multiple images.

Step 4: Play this visualization regularly to yourself and immediately before you make love.

—————————————————————— xxx ——————————————————————

You could also try setting anchors. As usual, it's best to have three different kinds of anchor – one visual, one auditory and one kinaesthetic. In this case, they'll all have to be under your control, both at the time of setting and at the time of firing.

HAVE A GO
Step 1: In your mind, see a previous occasion when you had amazing sex with your partner.

Step 2: Build your excitement (you can stimulate yourself physically as well as mentally, if you wish).

Step 3: Just *before* your excitement reaches a peak, set your anchors.

Step 4: Create a break state by thinking of something completely non-sexual.

Step 5: Repeat Steps 1–4 as many times as you feel necessary.

Step 6: Fire the anchors to see what happens. If you become aroused then it's worked. If not, go through the procedure again and again on other days.

Step 7: Once the anchors are established, future pace by visualizing scenes in which you successfully fire your anchors with your partner.

Step 8: Have sex with your partner using the anchors.

Self-hypnosis for performance anxiety

The Betty Erickson self-hypnosis method can also be used to help you overcome performance anxiety and make love more confidently and successfully. If you've forgotten how to put yourself into a trance, refer back to Chapter 1. When you're stating the purpose of your self-hypnosis (Step 3), say something like: 'I am entering into a trance for the purpose of allowing my unconscious mind to make the adjustments that will help me feel more confident in my lovemaking.' When you come to the visualization (Steps 5f and 5g), imagine a scene in which you are behaving in the way you want.

Breaking up is not so hard to do

NLP can help you improve your relationship and stay together, but there's absolutely no point using NLP or anything else to try to convince yourself that incompatibility is a fine basis for a relationship. Some relationships must come to an end and, when they do, one partner is often unable to accept the situation.

What should you do if you've been 'dumped' and can't get over it? Here's a technique that can help. It's the opposite of the *Love Story* technique described above. I call it the *Goodbye Story*.

HAVE A GO

Step 1: Instead of making yourself miserable by thinking about all the nice things associated with the person who dumped you, think instead of the *bad* things. There must have been some. Think of how your partner looked first thing in the morning. Think of your ex's worst physical aspects: the rolls of fat, the wrinkles round the neck, the sagging flesh, whatever it might be. Think of the times your partner let you down. Think of the worst thing your partner ever did to you. Carry on until you have five 'Worst Of' memories.

Step 2: Analyse each of the five scenes like a film director. What things could you do to increase their impact? Experiment with the submodalities. Maybe a close-up of the bags under the eyes?

Maybe louder volume for that row? Maybe some soundtrack music that you hate? Really put time and effort into this. Experience each scene to the maximum.

Step 3: Once you're satisfied with your five scenes, make them into a movie by running them one after another without a break. Then run the whole movie again a bit faster. Then run it faster still. Then yet again.

Step 4: Future pace. Visualize meeting your ex and feeling *nothing*. Certainly not love or desire, but not anger or hatred either. Having overcome a break-up in this way doesn't mean you have to be vindictive. In fact, you'll probably feel a lot more reasonable as you begin to feel less emotional. If you no longer care very much, then you've succeeded. Otherwise repeat the whole exercise on a daily basis until you're 'cured'.

Insight

Creating negative visualizations about your ex can be a powerful tool. For even greater impact also create positive visualizations about the new person you're hoping to meet, so you have something to look forward to. Don't make the positive visualization too specific (fair hair, high-powered job or whatever) or you'll possibly spoil your chances of meeting the right person. Just use the positive visualization as a way of remaining optimistic.

10 THINGS TO REMEMBER

1 *You can increase your loving feelings by visualizing five wonderful scenes from your life together and putting them together as your very own* Love Story.

2 *You can increase the love you project by using the Circle of Love.*

3 *The Swish technique can help you recreate the feelings you had right back in the beginning.*

4 *Modelling successful couples will always have something useful to teach you.*

5 *When you have a disagreement, never make things worse by recalling previous disagreements; instead switch perceptual positions and use matching and mirroring to re-establish rapport.*

6 *The Romantic Behaviour Generator can be used for everything from being more empathetic to being a better lover.*

7 *You can add variety to your love life by creating new anchors that make you both feel romantic or sexy.*

8 *It's possible to increase the sensitivity of erogenous zones or even create new ones using the Swish technique and anchoring.*

9 *Performance anxiety can be overcome using anchors and self-hypnosis.*

10 *Breaking-up can be less painful if you use the* Goodbye Story.

HOW AM I GETTING ON?

▶ *Have you made your very own* Love Story *movie in five scenes?*

▶ *Have you created a Circle of Love?*

▶ *Have you Swished and did you recover that 'walking on air' feeling?*

▶ *Have you modelled at least one couple?*

▶ *Have you stopped having rows and sulking afterwards?*

▶ *Have you been able to install at least one new romantic behaviour in yourself?*

▶ *Did you correctly guess at least ten of your partner's romantic and sexual anchors?*

▶ *Have you begun adding at least six new romantic/sexual anchors to your existing ones?*

▶ *Have you created a new erogenous area for yourself as well as for your partner?*

▶ *Are you feeling more relaxed about making love?*

If you answered 'No' to four or more questions, read through the relevant parts of the chapter once more and try the techniques again. Love may be natural but it's also a skill that can be improved.

NLP and hypnosis

In this chapter you will learn:
- *what hypnosis really is*
- *how you can hypnotize someone*
- *how NLP and hypnosis are closely connected.*

People already have all the resources they need.

NLP presupposition

When Richard Bandler and John Grinder gave seminars together one of them would say, 'All communication is hypnosis' and the other would say, 'Hypnosis doesn't exist'.

And both statements were, in different ways, right. So what *are* we talking about when we talk about hypnosis?

Stage hypnosis

Let's first of all deal with stage hypnosis – which is where most people get their preconceived ideas from. Derren Brown, the mentalist entertainer, says he doesn't really know himself what hypnosis is. He describes four types of volunteer:

▶ *the type who, encouraged by the hypnotist, fakes the whole thing*
▶ *the type who, pressurized by the situation, fakes the whole thing*

- *the type who, for the experience, tries hard to be hypnotized but knows he or she can end it at any time*
- *the type who relishes the permission given by the hypnotist to act outrageously.*

You'll note that none of those four cases seems like 'real' hypnotism.

In fact, I find I can hypnotize people very easily. For example, I was at a dinner party recently and I asked someone if they could please pass me the salt. And this is what happened. The person I was addressing reached out and grasped the salt cellar and handed it to me.

Now let me tell you about an occasion on which *I* was hypnotized. A friend spoke just nine words to me and, as a result, I spent the next year acting in a way exactly aligned with what he wanted. The words were, 'I challenge you to run a marathon with me.' And it was extremely hard work. What he got me to do was far, far more than anything any stage hypnotist has ever got anybody to do.

Presumably you're now jumping up and down and saying these are not examples of hypnosis. You think I'm ridiculous for even suggesting it. All that happened in the case of the salt was that I made a perfectly reasonable request with which the other person was happy to comply. And as for the marathon, obviously, I must have been already very willing to give it a go.

So when someone in a stage show asks a volunteer to prance around barking like a dog, why does everyone start talking about hypnosis?

In a sense, it's not the volunteer on stage who has been 'hypnotized' but the *audience*. Members of the audience see something perfectly ordinary (for example, a man becoming so relaxed that he slumps down into a chair) and yet believe they have seen something miraculous. Suppose that, instead of all the paraphernalia of hypnosis, the entertainer simply said, 'Thank you for coming up on stage. Please would you now hop around on one leg.' In all probability, most people would comply.

The greatest skill of stage hypnotists is not hypnosis but knowing how to select those members of the audience who want to entertain everyone else. A simple test prior to the show is to ask volunteers to hold out their hands, palms up, and imagine they have helium balloons tied to their right hands and lead weights to their left hands. Those whose hands remain at the same level are less suggestible than those whose hands move higher and lower.

What 'hypnosis' does in these circumstances is give people *permission* to loon about in front of an audience and thus to become, for a while, the centre of attention. For many people that's an intoxicating idea.

So now let's look at the genuine thing.

Real hypnosis

Milton Erickson – whose presence has permeated so much of this book – described hypnosis as 'the evocation and utilization of unconscious learning'.

In *Hypnotherapy – An Exploratory Casebook*, Erickson and co-author Ernest L. Rossi wrote that the value of hypnosis in psychotherapy is that it specifically helps people 'utilize their own mental associations, memories and life potentials' to achieve their own 'therapeutic goals'. It has nothing whatsoever to do with taking control of someone's mind, brainwashing or imposing ideas, and it certainly can't give people abilities they don't already possess (and especially not paranormal or superhuman ones). What hypnosis can do is help people utilize 'abilities and potentials that already exist within... but that remain unused or underdeveloped'.

It's this philosophy that gave rise to the NLP presupposition quoted at the start of the chapter, that people already have the resources they need.

It is hoped that you're already experiencing trance states on a regular basis, using the Betty Erickson method described in Chapter 1. In which case you're beginning to have an insight into what hypnosis is all about. So you'll know that a trance is not something extraordinary. In fact, while you're reading this and barely aware of what's going on around you you're in a trance state. When you're concentrating on throwing a ball you're in a trance state. When you're making love you're in a trance state.

And you've probably also realized by now that many NLP techniques are themselves simply forms of self-hypnosis by another name. The Fast Phobia Technique, for example, is a way of inducing a trance state. In fact, all visualizations are, by definition, trance states.

According to Erickson and Rossi: 'Therapeutic trance is a period during which the limitations of one's usual frames of reference and beliefs are temporarily altered…'.

So in this chapter we're going to, as it were, tackle hypnosis overtly rather than in the guise of NLP. We're going to call it by its name and you're going to learn how to hypnotize other people. Why should you do that? And why should anyone let you? Well, for example, through hypnosis, you might be able to help someone:

▶ *relax*
▶ *feel less anxious*
▶ *sleep better*
▶ *reduce pain*
▶ *have more confidence about something they have to do.*

Of course, there are other ways of helping people to tackle these issues. You could tell someone who is anxious, 'Don't worry – I'll sort it out'. And, very often, that will be comforting. But there can come a point at which the conscious mind can no longer see a way out. The conscious mind is far more limited than the unconscious. If you need to get a new concept across, if you need an expansion of horizons, then you have to speak to 'the wild part' – that's to say, the unconscious. Hypnosis is a good way to do it.

Learning hypnosis

According to Milton Erickson and Ernest Rossi, there is a 'five-stage paradigm of the dynamics of trance induction' that goes like this:

1 **Fixation of Attention** *via utilizing the patient's beliefs and behaviour for focusing attention on inner realities.*
2 **Depotentiating Habitual Frameworks and Belief Systems** *via distraction, shock, surprise, doubt, confusion, dissociation, or any other process that interrupts the patient's habitual frameworks.*
3 **Unconscious Search** *via implications, questions, puns, and other indirect forms of hypnotic suggestion.*
4 **Unconscious Process** *via activation of personal associations and mental mechanisms by all of the above.*
5 **Hypnotic Response** *via an expression of behavioural potentials that are experienced as taking place autonomously.*

But that's making the whole thing sound a lot more complicated than it really is. In fact, you probably have hypnotized someone *already* without realizing it. Have you, for example, ever told children a bedtime story so skilfully that they visualized everything that happened? That's hypnosis. Have you ever made a child's pain go away by 'kissing it better'? That's hypnosis. Have you ever soothed someone's fears by telling them, 'Don't worry – in a week's time you'll look back on this and laugh'? That's hypnosis. All we're going to do now is learn how to take that process just a little bit further. And when you get down to the practical methods it's a lot easier than Erickson and Rossi made it sound.

CHOOSING A SUBJECT

The best way to learn hypnosis is to find someone who is as curious as you are. Then you can learn together. Obviously, it's going to be much harder with someone who is reluctant. Here's an important tip:

Take both roles.

That's to say, don't just practise being the hypnotist. Also let the other person hypnotize you. You'll then have a far greater understanding of what works and what doesn't.

Despite the popular notion that 'you can't be hypnotized against your will', very skilled and resourceful hypnotists can hypnotize just about anybody (if necessary, turning their resistance against themselves). But as far as you're concerned, when it comes to using your newly-acquired skills to help people it's only going to work if they're willing to cooperate. Explain that you'd like to help them and that you need their active collaboration. In fact, this is the normal situation when someone consults a hypnotherapist.

As Erickson and Rossi wrote: 'A singularly important aspect of this optimal attitude is *expectancy*. Patients' expectations of therapeutic change permits [sic] them to suspend the learned limitations and negative life experiences that are at the source of their problems.'

IS IT DANGEROUS?

When you first think about hypnotizing other people, you'll probably feel excitement and curiosity but also anxiety about unleashing traumas that have been repressed, getting someone 'stuck' in a trance and generally 'messing about' with other people's minds. In fact, these *are* real dangers but they're avoidable as long as you behave responsibly and limit yourself to things within your competence.

Keep in mind that putting someone into a trance is not the same thing as depriving them of control. The unconscious mind is very protective. Professional hypnotists say that, under hypnosis, it's often harder to get someone to do something that's potentially harmful to them than if they were in a normal waking state. (Just think, for example, of the crazy things some people agree to do when they're 'normal', such as drink from every bottle in a bar, inhale carcinogenic smoke or lie in the sun until they're bright red!)

IS IT ETHICAL?

It's perfectly ethical to hypnotize someone, provided you've agreed beforehand what the aim of the hypnosis is to be and it's something sensible and worthwhile. Make those NLP ecology checks before proceeding. In other words, any change you're hoping to make must be positive for every aspect of the subject and for everyone else affected.

HOW TO SPEAK

What you say is obviously very important, but it's also crucial *how* you say it. No doubt you've seen films in which hypnotists speak in a very deep voice. It's not exactly that a deep voice is essential (if it were, there would be very few women hypnotists) but that irritating voices – and that includes high-pitched voices – work counter to the trance state. Your voice needs to be *soothing*. You yourself need to be *relaxed* and when you're relaxed, your voice tends to be deeper quite naturally.

But there is another rather different point. It's helpful to have one voice for being 'normal' and another voice for being 'hypnotic'. Making your voice deeper is a signal. Once anyone associates a deep voice with a trance state (and thanks to films most of us do) then using a deep voice makes success more likely. Moreover, if someone has been put into trance by a deep voice, so using that tone of voice on subsequent occasions can induce trance almost automatically.

Other ways of signalling that you require a trance state include changes in your posture and style. You could also ask your partner to sit in a special place for hypnosis – a 'hypnosis chair' as it were.

There is one other reason for having these signals. Not only do they facilitate future sessions but they help prevent your partner going into trance when it's *not* intended. The fact is, when someone has learned to go into trance, it becomes easier and easier. As a result, you might inadvertently put them into trance when it's not planned. However, if the other person has been programmed to go into trance *only* when you use a special voice (and possibly other signals) then 'accidental hypnosis' won't occur.

Your voice also needs to be *confident*. No one is going to entrust themselves to the care of someone whose own voice betrays doubts about the whole thing. You can help overcome anxiety on your part by remembering that it's not your job to *make* your partner go into trance. It's not a battle of wills. Your task is to help your partner go into trance *if she or he wants to*. You're *working together*.

Tempo is another key factor, as we saw in Chapters 1 and 7. Note the other person's breathing and match your phrases accordingly. That's to say... break up the phrases... so one part... of a phrase... goes with the... breathing in... and the next... goes with the... breathing out... and so on... and on. Then you can gradually... slow down... and slow down... and your partner... will follow... your lead... and breathe... more slowly... and become... more relaxed... and deeper... and deeper... in trance...

Finally, you need to be aware of emphasis, or what hypnotists call 'analogue marking'. This is when you change your voice tone or use a gesture to mark certain words that are especially important. John Grinder tells a story about having a woman come to see him who would wake in the night sweating and vibrating and nobody had been able to work out what was wrong. The woman told Grinder how she would 'switch off the *electric* light' and lie down, and how she found it 'very *shocking*' because she had been 'in *treatment* for years'. Grinder had the sensitivity to pick up on the analogue markings and realized that at some point she'd been through electric shock treatment. None of the people who had been treating her recently had known this but, with this insight, Grinder was able to help her.

In this case, it was the client who was doing the analogue marking. But you, as the hypnotist, can also use it to draw the attention of the unconscious to the ideas you want to plant. The most sophisticated way of doing this is by using 'embedded commands'. These are commands that are 'hidden' in the way that objects are hidden in some kinds of picture puzzles. For example, supposing you were to say:

> *'I would like you to bring me the file next to the coffee machine.'*

Then, indeed, you should get the file you want. But you could say it like this, using analogue marking for the underlined words:

> *'I would like you to <u>bring me</u> the file next to the <u>coffee</u> machine.'*

In that case, with a bit of luck, you might get a cup of coffee along with the file. Of course, the fact that a command is embedded doesn't mean it *will* be carried out. But embedded commands have a way of working on the unconscious that can add to the effect of other techniques you're using and may sometimes be effective on their own.

PRACTISING THE BASIC SKILLS

I'm assuming you're going to start out by experimenting on someone you know quite well and who is as curious as you are. Even so, you may never have noticed whether or not they favour a particular representational system – that's to say, whether they mostly 'see' things in their minds, or 'hear' them or 'feel' them. (If you've forgotten about primary representational systems turn back to Chapters 1 and 7.) If you don't know, establish it first by asking them to describe something they've experienced and pay attention to the language they use. Once you know, **your own language should favour the subject's primary representational system, unless the subject is comfortable with all three main representational systems, in which case you can use any of them.**

Ask your collaborator to think of an activity that tends to create 'a world of its own' and say what it is in a word or short phrase. Tell them not to give more information than necessary – just 'swimming' or 'listening to music' or 'jogging' or whatever. Then ask them to close their eyes and imagine it. Your job is now to describe what you think is going on in their internal cinema in such a way that it deepens their experience. For example, you might say: 'You feel the coolness of the water on your skin' (kinaesthetic); 'You hear the steady rhythm' (auditory) or 'You see your hands moving in time with your steps' (visual).

After a couple of minutes of this, stop and discuss what things seemed to help towards creating a trance state and what things damaged it. Then change roles.

Insight

What you'll find is that when you say things that match the other person's internal experience, they begin to go 'deeper'. But when you say things that jar, the other person begins to 'come out' of the visualization. You'll realize that you need to confine yourself to things that *have* to be in the experience, that are *universal*. For example, if you say, 'You're thinking how nice the countryside is', that may or may not be the case. So that's the kind of thing to avoid. But if you say to someone who is visualizing jogging, 'You feel the rhythmical movement of your hips' then that *has* to match their experience. So that's the kind of thing you need to say.

Method 1: a simple technique for inducing hypnosis

The idea of this technique is to feed back to people things that they're experiencing. In other words, you'll be 'pacing' and then 'leading' in the way you've hopefully been practising since Chapter 7. The norm is to make three or more pacing statements before every leading statement. And you'll be favouring the primary representational system or, for those who don't especially have one, using all three main systems.

To help you understand, here are some short examples together with explanatory comments:

> *'Your name is Jeremy... and you're 28 years old. Very good. Now, as you sit in that comfortable red chair... your feet... on the floor... your hands... feeling the smoothness... of the armrests... and hearing my voice... so I'd like you to...'.*

Did you spot the pacing statements? Jeremy knows that everything you have said is true: he is Jeremy, he is 28, he is sitting in the red chair and he can hear your voice. So when you go on to make a suggestion Jeremy will be quite open to it. He will assume that it, too, will be 'true' because it's part of a pattern. You'll magnify the effect when you introduce things the other person wouldn't normally notice, and it helps if they're at the interface of the body and the environment. So it's useful to say, for example, 'You see your hands', but it's even more powerful to say, 'Your hands are feeling the smoothness of the armrests'. Did you also notice that all three representational systems were used in this case?

> *'...so I'd like you to notice how you're starting to feel relaxed. So relaxed that you're beginning to drift away into a kind of sleep.'*

You've already met this kind of presupposition (in Chapter 7). A presupposition, in this context, simply means speaking about something as if the other person already knows it or already agrees. You could simply have said, 'You are feeling sleepy' but that would have been far less effective.

The 'as you ... so' construction (which began in the first example and concluded in this one) is what's known as a transition because it takes the subject into the trance. Words such as 'while', 'when', 'because' and 'and' can all also be used to create transitions.

There are three levels of linkage:

▶ X and Y. *For example: 'You sit in that chair and you begin to relax.'*
▶ As X, Y. *For example: 'As you sit in that chair you begin to relax.'*
▶ X *causes* Y. *For example: 'The comfort of the chair will cause you to relax.'*

The point is that there's no actual connection between sitting in the chair and relaxing (you can sit in a chair and be tense), but the use of the transition words links the two ideas and makes it seem that there's a logical progression from one thing to the next. For brevity, I've kept this example and the preceding one short but, in practice, you'll probably have to continue your use of pacing, leading and presupposition for a while before getting a response.

SOME REFINEMENTS

'Until I say this you will be unaware of the feeling of warmth in the small of your back. And as that warmth spreads out, so your feeling of relaxation may intensify.'

Your subject will be forced to shift attention to the small of the back and will then notice the warmth. This does two things. It gives you credibility because you were right. And it changes their awareness. Of course, you don't have to refer to the back. You can do something similar with other parts of the body.

The word 'may' is known as a 'modal operator of possibility'. Other examples are 'might' and 'could'. The point of them is that you don't ever want your subject to 'fail' so you don't say something definitely *will* happen.

'You don't have to go into trance until you are really ready.'

This combines two things we learned about in Chapter 7, the use of a negative to discharge resistance and the use of presupposition; you, as hypnotist, are taking it as definite that the subject *will* go into trance at some point. Other useful kinds of negatives are, 'You can't stop it, can you?' and 'Why not let that happen?'

> *'And the next time your eyes begin to close, you could simply allow them to stay shut.'*

Calibrating carefully, you feed back someone's reactions to them and make it seem as if *you* have *caused* the changes. This is known as 'incorporation'. Incorporation means using something somebody is *already* doing. So as soon as you see eyes closing you say, 'And as your eyes begin to close…' Or it might be: 'As you blink your eyes…'; 'As you cross your ankles…'; 'As you let your head drop forwards…'. When you use incorporation you give the impression of having great insight.

> *'That's right, that's right.'*

It's important to let people know they're doing well. But these words of encouragement also have another function which is, again, to establish confidence in your skill. For example, if you suggest a visualization and then see signs of eye movement behind closed eyelids, then you'll know the subject is probably visualizing. By saying, 'That's right' you both encourage them to go deeper and make it seem that you are someone with special knowledge.

> *'Okay, we're at level 3, now we're going to level 4.'*

Confirming the state gives confidence to the subject. At the outset you might say that on a scale of one to ten (with one as the normal waking state) you'll be aiming to take your subject as deep as seven. That gives a target to aim at – but one that's not too intimidating.

> *'I'd like you to raise a finger when you've reached level 5.'*

Feedback is important to you as the hypnotist but also to the subject. It makes the subject play an active role in their own hypnosis.

> *'And as you hear the sound of that car starting up and driving away so, as it recedes into the distance, you, too, go further and deeper...'*

This kind of thing is a device for dealing with interruptions that can so easily occur. In this case it's a car but it might also be a telephone, a doorbell or someone unexpectedly coming into the room. Just calmly incorporate the interruption into your pacing and leading.

> *'I wonder if you dare go deeper...'*

It's seldom a good idea to 'order' your subject to do anything, because that might create resentment. This kind of construction, using 'I wonder', overcomes resistance. If you think 'dare' might be too strong for your subject, try 'I wonder if you have the ability to go deeper into trance...'.

> *'As your hands rest ever so lightly on your thighs, do you notice how they tend to lift up a bit all by themselves with each breath you take?'*

Once again, rather than 'order' the subject, you try a roundabout method, in this case asking a question, '...do you notice...'. This particular example usually forms a preamble to 'hand levitation' in which the subject is then asked, 'Does one hand or the other or maybe both continue lifting even more?' This, you'll notice, is a 'bind' as described in Chapter 7.

More methods of inducing hypnosis

Pacing and leading is a standard technique but there are many others. In reality, you probably won't use just one technique but a combination, depending on the way your subject is responding.

HYPNOSIS METHOD NUMBER 2

The handshake induction is a famous way of putting someone in a trance. The way it works is rather intriguing. We all have certain behaviours programmed into us as a unit which the professionals call a TOTE. Have you, for example, ever learned to play a piece of music? Then you've probably had the experience that if you can't remember the first two or three notes you can't remember any of it. And yet as soon as the first few notes come back to you, you can play the whole piece without a problem. That's because you learned the music as a unit, as a TOTE, and the whole of that behaviour is now performed without conscious thought.

Here's what you do for the handshake induction:

▶ *Hold out your right hand as if to shake hands.*
▶ *The other person advances his or her right hand.*
▶ *Intercept the person's hand with your left hand and sharply pull the forearm into a vertical position.*
▶ *You're now at a (psychological) leverage point. Immediately lead that person into trance, using the kind of language you've already learned.*

Jargon buster – leverage point

A **leverage point** is a moment at which another person is totally confused and you have the possibility to lead that person where you wish them to go. In the case of the handshake induction, you've stopped someone in the middle of a piece of automatic behaviour and, for a few short moments, they don't know how to proceed. They're therefore susceptible to any voice of authority.

HYPNOSIS METHOD NUMBER 3

When someone goes on and on about something you find rather boring, you undoubtedly glaze over. Well, that is a kind of trance and you can exploit that effect. What you do is talk at length and monotonously about situations in which natural trances occur, such as driving a car, or watching television, or riding in a train or a lift. For example:

'I had just left my house... in my car... and it was a wet afternoon... with the windscreen wipers... slowly moving... backwards and forwards... and I was thinking... about a problem... I had... and...'

HYPNOSIS METHOD NUMBER 4

Ask questions that require your subject to visualize a scene from childhood. For example, 'Can you describe to me the house about which you have your earliest memories?' If the answer is very superficial then you can prompt with questions such as, 'Can you describe the wallpaper you had in your bedroom?'

HYPNOSIS METHOD NUMBER 5

When a person's conscious mind is overloaded with information or with tasks so it can't register any more, then any 'overflow' goes into the unconscious without the conscious mind being aware of it. So here's what you do. Ask your subject to count backwards out loud from 200 in threes, with eyes closed, while you place your hands on their shoulders and turn them in circles. Then tell them, 'If at any time you find it more comfortable to go into a trance please do so in the knowledge that you are in safe hands.' At some point the person will probably go into a trance.

Insight

An advantage of this method is that you have feedback. If your subject stops counting, it means they've either gone into trance or have escaped the disorientation. If they've escaped, simply ask them to continue counting. Otherwise you can make your suggestions.

HYPNOSIS METHOD NUMBER 6

The idea of this method is also to overload a person's conscious mind – in this case with stories within stories within stories within stories – so they eventually give up trying to keep track of which reality is being spoken about at any moment. For that reason it's known as 'stacking realities'. Try saying something along the following lines:

> *'As you sit there... I want you to notice... the tops of the trees... moving backwards... and forwards... in the wind... because a friend of mine... sat in that very chair... last week... and as she sat... watching those trees... swaying... this way and that... and listening to the sound... of my voice... so she went... into a deep reverie... and remembered a dream... about seeing exactly... those kinds of trees... on a day out... in the countryside... when it was very warm... and pleasant... and she lay down... in the shade... of the trees... and fell asleep... and something happened... while she was asleep... that changed her... and at first... she didn't know...'*

HYPNOSIS METHOD NUMBER 7

Mirroring your subject is always a good thing to do because the more you establish rapport, the more likely you are to succeed. This technique actually uses mirroring to lead someone right into trance. Begin by mirroring things such as posture and breathing until you feel you have rapport, and then slowly and gradually make some changes to see if your subject follows your lead. If so, go into trance yourself (you already know about this through the Betty Erickson method) and your subject should do the same.

Insight
Erickson would sometimes go into a trance with clients in order to be more sensitive.

Knowing when someone is in a trance

Quite often people will deny that they were in a trance. Perhaps you have yourself been to see a hypnotist and weren't sure if you were in a trance or not. So are there any ways that you, as a hypnotist, can be sure you've succeeded? Here are some signs that are consistent with a trance state:

▶ *face muscles relax and the face gets flatter*
▶ *there may be little twitches*
▶ *breathing changes*
▶ *muscle relaxation leads to increased blood flow to the extremities, for example warm hands*
▶ *eyes might roll up (but someone can be in a trance with eyes open)*
▶ *closed eyelids flickering are indicative that visualization is taking place.*

WHAT NOW?

So your subject is in a trance. What do you do now? As I emphasized earlier, you should agree the aim of the hypnosis at the outset. If you're both just learning and experimenting you, as hypnotist, could say something like this 'process instruction':

> '...and you can allow... your unconscious... to present to you... a memory... that will give you... great delight... something you had forgotten... which will come back... to you... when I bring you... out of your trance...'

Insight

Asking the unconscious to retrieve some pleasant memories that had been forgotten is an enjoyable use of hypnosis. The unconscious can sort through memories much faster than the conscious. 'Mining' the past in this way can help some people be happier now.

Obviously, you shouldn't attempt to do anything that's outside your competence. Nor should you be attempting to find out personal things or delve into the roots of personality problems. Remember that NLP takes the view that it's not normally necessary to know *why* someone is the way they are, rather how they *stay* that way – and what they want to achieve.

Problems in hypnosis

It's very unlikely that you'll put someone into a trance in which they get stuck. However, if they don't 'wake up' then the solution is to pace them to re-establish rapport and lead them once again back to normal consciousness. One way is to get very close and match your breathing to the other person's, letting your breath fall on the other person's ear. After two or three minutes try changing your breathing and the other person should follow.

Sometimes it happens that, through hypnosis, someone gains access to unpleasant memories that had been repressed and, perhaps, begins to cry. This is known as abreaction. The response is to acknowledge what's going on, then add a context reframe:

> *'You are crying… and those tears… are representative of pain and discomfort… in your past… but I would like you to consider… that we all have painful experiences… and that they often form… the basis for the development… of later skills and strengths… which people who have never… been challenged… do not develop.'*

You could also use dissociation:

> *'You can now… look back at yourself… as you were… at that time… and feel proud… that you survived… that experience… and were strengthened by it.'*

Better still would be to avoid abreaction altogether until you have more experience. Before you begin you could say:

> *'It is the role... of your unconscious mind... to protect you... from memories that are painful... or overwhelming... and I call upon... your unconscious mind... now... to continue to perform that role... so that as you alter... your consciousness... so you will... for the time being... only access memories... that will please and delight you.'*

The NLP connection

By now it should be fairly clear that much of NLP is what might be called 'hypnosis lite'. In *Hypnotherapy – An Exploratory Casebook*, Erickson and Rossi argued that people have problems because of 'learned limitations'. They're caught in 'mental sets, frames of reference, and belief systems that do not permit them to explore and utilize their own abilities to best advantage'. The job of the therapist is to identify those false limitations and guide the client towards 'new horizons'. Excitingly, Erickson and Rossi wrote that all human beings are still in the process of learning to use their potentials. Who knows how far we can all go?

NLP, too, has the aim of helping people learn to use their potentials. It uses many of the same ideas and processes but without the hypnosis. As Bandler and Grinder wrote in *Trance-formations*, 'there's nothing you can do with a person in trance that you can't do with a person out of trance'.

In the next chapter you'll find a structured plan to help you achieve *your* potential, using all the things you've learned in this book.

10 THINGS TO REMEMBER

1 *NLP derives many of its techniques from those used in hypnotherapy.*

2 *Don't judge hypnosis by the kinds of things you see on television or stage shows.*

3 *Hypnosis is 'the evocation and utilization of unconscious learning'.*

4 *Trance is a common experience – one definition of therapeutic trance is that it's simply a period when the limitations of one's usual frames of reference and beliefs are temporarily altered.*

5 *The technique of pacing and leading is a standard way of inducing trance.*

6 *It's important to give your subject encouragement and helpful to provide a mechanism for feedback, such as raising a finger.*

7 *A TOTE is a behaviour that has been learned as a unit, such that interrupting it causes confusion and a leverage point.*

8 *When someone is at a leverage point, they can often be led in the direction you wish them to go.*

9 *Signs that someone is in trance may include flatter features, changes in breathing, warmer hands, eyes rolled up or closed eyelids flickering.*

10 *The purpose of hypnosis should be agreed at the outset – for example, it could be the recalling of a delightful memory.*

HOW AM I GETTING ON?

▶ *Have you and a friend begun exploring hypnosis together?*

▶ *Have you been able to develop a 'hypnotic voice' that's relaxed, confident and in time with your subject's breathing?*

▶ *Have you been able to emphasize key points or even create embedded commands by analogue marking?*

▶ *Have you been able to say things that helped someone go deeper into a visualization?*

▶ *Have you been able to use pacing and leading, together with a transition, to put someone into trance?*

▶ *By using calibration, have you been able to make it seem as if you caused physical changes in a subject that were in fact, natural?*

▶ *Have you been able to cause 'hand levitation'?*

▶ *Have you tried the handshake induction?*

▶ *Are you comfortable with at least four ways of inducing trance?*

▶ *Do you know how to deal with someone stuck in trance or who is having a traumatic experience (abreaction)?*

You may have been sufficiently inspired to have a go at hypnotizing a willing friend. And it's important that you should also let your friend have a go at hypnotizing you. It's all part of learning what works and what doesn't. Quite quickly you should be able to deepen a friend's visualization and – if you practise the speech patterns conscientiously – then you should be able to hypnotize anyone who is cooperative.

10

Your NLP four-week action plan

In this chapter you will learn:
* *how to plan your personal development*
* *how to turn wasted time into worthwhile time*
* *how 28 days can transform your life.*

   Choice is better than no choice.

NLP presupposition

Your first step is to plan out how you wish to be and in what ways you want your life to be transformed. Be as precise as possible. Vague aims such as 'I'll improve my relationship with my partner', 'I'll earn more money' or 'I'll get better at golf' are unlikely to be very successful. You need clear and, wherever possible, measurable goals and specific plans for achieving them. For example: 'I'm going to improve my health through daily exercise with a target of reducing my resting heart rate by four beats a minute at the end of one month' or, 'I'm going to increase my self-confidence through NLP visualization techniques and apply for a management position in two weeks.'

Take out your diary, or a wall chart, and decide a realistic time frame for what you have in mind. As we saw in Chapter 5, it's a good idea to work backwards from your goal. So use the 'reverse engineering' visualization and mark off the key stages and dates. Here we're working to four weeks, which is enough time to achieve some important goals. But of course, not everything can be achieved in a month, so adapt the plan as necessary.

Day 1

The first day is all about making plans and discovering new things about yourself.

▶ *Mark out your timetable in your diary or on a wall chart.*

▶ *Work out if your motivation is generally away from unpleasant things or towards enjoyable things (Chapter 5), then use that knowledge to design ways of motivating yourself more effectively.*

▶ *Work out if you have a primary representational system (Chapter 1).*

▶ *Work out the way you code time (your 'timeline') and then rearrange the sequence of selected memories, bringing enjoyable memories forward and pushing bothersome memories back into the distant past (Chapter 2).*

▶ *Memorize the NLP presuppositions (Chapter 1).*

▶ *Identify a person you would like to model and make a plan for dealing with the practical considerations.*

▶ *Begin a healthy living routine. Use the Swish technique to motivate yourself to exercise regularly (Chapter 6). Find a picture of the kind of body you'd like to have and pin it up somewhere you can see it every day.*

▶ *On a small piece of card, make a list of all the great things your partner does for you and put it in a safe place in your bag or wallet so you can refer to it if you have a row.*

Any day you have the opportunity

You'll never be bored when you're using NLP to transform your life because there are so many skills to be practising. Sitting on a train or in a waiting room, you can keep yourself completely entertained with nothing other than your own senses and your mind.

- ▶ *Call up one of the presuppositions and think about it. Remember, the idea of the NLP presuppositions is not that they're necessarily true but that they're useful. Ask yourself: 'In what way can I use this presupposition to move my life forward?'*
- ▶ *Practise your visualization skills (Chapter 2). Make your internal cinema as rich as you possibly can by employing all the techniques you've ever seen at the real cinema. Try swapping images so rapidly (Swishing) that the emotions attached to the first image become transferred to the second.*
- ▶ *Work on compiling the mental library of anecdotes and stories you will use to pass on advice in a subtle way (Chapter 7). A book such as* My Voice Will Go With You *(Chapter 11) will give you plenty of ideas.*
- ▶ *Calibrate everyone you can (Chapter 7). That's to say, observe body language and relate it to people's emotions – especially any caused by you. Particularly watch for eye movements when you put questions to people. Is there a pattern?*
- ▶ *When you're alone, practise speaking in your 'hypnotic voice' (Chapter 9); that is, confident, relaxed, probably deeper than usual, and at the tempo of breathing.*

Every bedtime

When you're drifting off to sleep is a good moment to program your unconscious.

- ▶ *Before you go to sleep each night, give yourself instructions for the way you'll feel when you wake up (Chapter 5). Something like: 'I'll wake up at 7.30 a.m. feeling completely refreshed and eager to get on with...'.*
- ▶ *Visualize yourself as healthy, even if you have health problems (Chapter 6).*
- ▶ *If you wake in the night and can't sleep, use the time enjoyably and creatively by 'watching' visualizations (Chapter 2).*

Every day

▶ *Talk to your inner voice just as if it's that of another person. Have a chat – apart from anything else, an inner voice can be good company. Make it a habit. Practise getting your inner voice to send you unambiguous signals. Once you're comfortable with that, use Six Step Reframing (Chapter 4) to discover the positive intention behind a negative inner voice and to develop alternative ways of achieving that positive intention.*

▶ *Make an effort to match and mirror people (Chapter 7). If you're clumsy and upset anyone, you can always explain that you're studying NLP. (But it might not be a good idea to match and mirror your boss until you've perfected your technique!)*

Week 1

▶ *Approach your model and seek their cooperation (Chapter 3).*

▶ *Try to enter a state of flow (Chapter 3).*

▶ *If you have a phobia, begin tackling it now with the Fast Phobia Technique (Chapter 2).*

▶ *Begin the task of taking control of your negative inner voice. Try discrediting it by making it sound exactly like someone you distrust (see Chapter 4). All this week, be alert for any negative instructions from your inner voice and get it to rephrase them in positive terms. In other words, if your inner voice is telling you, 'Don't be anxious about...' then it needs to rephrase as, 'You can feel completely confident about...'.*

▶ *Boost your confidence with the Circle of Confidence (Chapter 5). Then, for good measure, Swish for confidence.*

▶ *Begin learning a new mental skill or improving an existing mental skill. Remind yourself how considerable your learning abilities are by visualizing how you learned to walk, speak, read and write as a child (Chapter 2).*

- Begin learning a new physical skill or improve an existing physical skill. As soon as possible, hand over to your unconscious (Chapter 2).

Weekend 1

- Use the Betty Erickson method to put yourself into a trance (Chapter 1). At this stage, tackle a fairly simple issue.
- Spend time making an internal movie of five romantic scenes from your life together with your partner (Chapter 8).

Week 2

- Is there something in the past over which you blame yourself for the way you behaved? If you have to think hard then skip this. But if there's something about your past behaviour that keeps bothering you then absolve yourself using the Decision Destroyer (Chapter 2).
- Whatever behaviour you'd like to have, turn it into an internal movie using the New Behaviour Generator (Chapter 5). Run it today and every day for the next week.
- Spend time with your model, absorbing everything your model does (preferably in a state of flow) and making a video (Chapter 2).
- Have a go at creating 'anchors' (Chapter 5). To begin with, stick to something simple – such as anchoring laughter.
- Practise the pain control techniques (Chapter 6) so that you have them available to you should you ever need them.
- Continue learning the new skills you started on in Week 1.
- If you've used the Fast Phobia Technique, continue exposing yourself to whatever you're frightened of.

Weekend 2

▶ *Use the Betty Erickson method to put yourself into a trance. With the experience you now have, tackle a more difficult issue than you did last weekend.*

▶ *Entertain friends at a party with your new palm reading skills (Chapter 7).*

▶ *Swish an image of your partner from the heady early days of your relationship with an image from today.*

Week 3

▶ *Every day this week, watch the video you made of your model (Chapter 2).*

▶ *If you have anything you'd like to give up (smoking, drinking too much, getting angry) think of five scenes when your behaviour was at its worst and make them into an internal film (Chapter 5).*

▶ *Create a set of anchors for relaxation (Chapter 6).*

▶ *Continue learning the new skills you started on in Weeks 1 and 2.*

▶ *If you've used the Fast Phobia Technique, increase your exposure to whatever you're frightened of.*

Weekend 3

▶ *Learn about hypnosis by asking an equally curious friend to visualize something. Your job is to deepen the visualization by describing what your friend is experiencing (Chapter 9). Then swap roles.*

- ▶ Use the Circle of Love to increase the love you project to your partner and everyone else (Chapter 8).
- ▶ Use the Romantic Behaviour Generator to install a new behaviour that will thrill your partner (Chapter 8).

Week 4

- ▶ Move into the explicit modelling phase by subtracting any aspects of your model's behaviour that you suspect are not contributing to the desired result (Chapter 3).
- ▶ Make a point of trying out the 'artfully vague' Milton Model (Chapter 7). Experiment with compound statements of cause and effect, pacing and leading, presuppositions, stories and quotes.
- ▶ You should now be very familiar with the Betty Erickson method (Chapter 1) and can use it whenever you need a little extra help or cooperation from your subconscious.
- ▶ Continue learning the new skills you started on in Weeks 1 to 3.
- ▶ If you've used the Fast Phobia Technique, take your exposure to whatever you're frightened of to the highest prudent level.

Weekend 4

- ▶ Have a go at hypnotizing a willing friend using the techniques of pacing, leading and presupposition (Chapter 9). Then let your friend try to hypnotize you. Experiment with other ways of inducing trance, such as the handshake induction.
- ▶ Spend some time discovering your partner's natural anchors for romance (Chapter 8). Try installing a few more anchors on your partner and let your partner install some new anchors on you.

Taking it further

If you'd like to learn more about NLP, there are various websites you can consult. Make a point of including one or two that are sceptical. There are some quite extravagant claims being made for NLP and it's important you should have a balanced view. Books are a relatively inexpensive starting point for serious study. Afterwards, if you feel you'd like to get practical experience, or would actually like to become an NLP practitioner, then you could start looking into courses.

One of the reasons NLP has grown so quickly is that it offers the possibility of being able to earn a living helping people, without first having to study for years and years. But beware of organizations claiming they can train you to a professional standard in as little as a weekend. Similarly, make sure the people who are going to be training you are, themselves, properly qualified.

Websites

www.nlpu.com
This site contains masses of material by Robert Dilts – a leading figure in NLP – as well as the Encyclopedia of NLP, which explains all the jargon.

www.Bradburyac.mistral.co.uk
Run by Andy Bradbury, author of *Develop Your NLP Skills*, this site includes articles, reviews, frequently asked questions and useful links.

www.mheap.com/nlp.html
Michael Heap, a clinical and forensic psychologist, takes issue with some of the claims for NLP.

Books

Richard Bandler and John Grinder *Frogs Into Princes* (Real People Press, 1979)
This is the book that really introduced Neuro-Linguistic Programming to the world and is actually the transcript of a live training session. On the plus side, that means it's practical and couched in more readable language than many other books in which Grinder has been involved. On the other hand, the organization of the material isn't always ideal. But if you're seriously interested in NLP, this is a seminal work from the men who created it and, therefore, essential reading.

Richard Bandler and John Grinder *The Structure of Magic, Volumes 1 & 2 (*Meta Publications, 1975)
The very first books from the Bandler/Grinder team, these two volumes are based largely on modelling the techniques used by the family therapist Virginia Satir and introduced the so-called Meta Model. Mainly of interest to therapists.

Richard Bandler and John Grinder *Patterns of the Hypnotic Techniques of Milton H. Erickson, Volume 1* (Meta Publications, 1975) and Richard Bandler, Judith DeLozier and John Grinder *Volume 2* (Meta Publications, 1977)
It was the modelling of the hypnotherapist Milton Erickson that gave NLP so many of its techniques. However, this two-volume work, just like *The Structure of Magic*, is written in such an academic way that it is unlikely to be of interest to non-professionals.

Richard Bandler and John Grinder *Trance-formations* (Real People Press, 1980)
This is one of the more readable books to result from the Bandler/Grinder collaboration. In essence, it's the transcript of a seminar on trance and hypnosis and is highly recommended for anyone who has a serious interest in the subject or who actually wants to become a hypnotist.

Milton H. Erickson and Ernest L. Rossi *Hypnotherapy – An Explanatory Casebook* (Irvington, 1979)

This is a much more readable account of Erickson's methods than Bandler and Grinder's *Patterns of the Hypnotic Techniques of Milton H. Erickson*. Rossi describes Erickson's techniques in plain language and includes transcripts of Erickson's actual words together with explanatory comments.

Sidney Rosen *My Voice Will Go With You – The Teaching Tales of Milton H. Erickson* (Norton, 1991)
The title of this book comes from a phrase that Erickson often included in his hypnotic inductions: 'And my voice will go with you wherever you are'. It enabled him to keep contact with a client, regardless of the depth of the trance. Many ex-patients found that Erickson's voice – or at least his stories – remained with them all their lives, because they were highly significant. This collection provides a valuable insight into Erickson's methods and a way of thinking that was often highly original and counter-intuitive.

Steve Andreas and Charles Faulkner *NLP – The New Technology of Achievement* (Nicholas Brealey, 1996)
This is very much about finding your role in life and achieving your goals, with an emphasis on NLP visualization techniques.

Steve Bavister and Amanda Vickers *Teach Yourself NLP* (Hodder Education, 2008)
A comprehensive and very readable description of everything in NLP, by two certified NLP coaches. A good book for anyone going on an NLP course.

Richard Bandler *Get The Life You Want* (HarperElement, 2008)
One of many books written by Bandler alone, this is a very easy read with simple NLP techniques.

John Grinder and Carmen Bostic St Clair *Whispering in the Wind* (self-published, 2001)
Grinder had always seen modelling as the core of NLP and, after the split from Bandler, he set about making it more his own by developing what he called New Code, at one point with Judith Delozier, and then with Carmen Bostic St Clair. Aimed at NLP professionals.

Joseph O'Connor *NLP Workbook* (Thorsons, 2001)
A practical and easily understood guide to most things in NLP.

Coaching

There are NLP coaches all over the world, specializing in all kinds
of things. If you would like to find an NLP practitioner near you,
you may find the following websites useful:

www.anlp.org
The website of the UK-based Association for Neuro-Linguistic
Programming, with a searchable database of practitioners.

www.bbnlp.com
Website of the British Board of NLP with a searchable database.

www.nlpschedule.com
Includes a database of NLP practitioners in the UK.

www.nlptca.com
The website of the Neuro Linguistic Psychotherapy and
Counselling Association in the UK, with a searchable directory of
members.

It's important to check what kind of training and experience an
NLP practitioner has. Standards can vary enormously. Have a
chat on the phone and don't commit yourself to anything beyond
the preliminary session so you'll have the chance to make up your
mind based on how that goes.

If you would actually like to train to become an NLP coach, you
may find the following websites of interest:

www.inlpta.co.uk
Website for the International NLP Trainers Association which has
members in over 20 countries.

www.johngrinder.co.uk
John Grinder is the co-founder of NLP and here you'll find details of his seminars in the UK.

www.johngrinder.com
Details of New Code NLP which was developed by John Grinder and others after he and Richard Bandler went their separate ways.

www.nlp.org
A seminar searcher.

www.ppdlearning.co.uk
Provides various courses for NLP professionals, including 21 days to become a practitioner – lecturers include leading names in NLP such as Robert Dilts, Joseph O'Connor, Judith DeLozier and Charles Faulkner.

www.professionalguildofnlp.com
Website of the Professional Guild of NLP which can provide details of training courses available.

www.richardbandler.com
Website of the co-creator of NLP.

Training courses vary considerably. It's attractive to think that you can help other people on the basis of a single weekend course but, realistically, you need to think in terms of something much longer. Online courses can seem a good idea but be careful you're not paying a large sum of money for information you could have obtained much more cheaply from books. When it comes to working with clients there's no substitute for practical training.

Index